We Wish to See Jesus

Pastor Dennis Thomas

WestBow
PRESS
A DIVISION OF THOMAS NELSON

Copyright © 2012 Pastor Dennis Thomas

All rights reserved. No part of this book may be used or reproduced by any means, graphic, electronic, or mechanical, including photocopying, recording, taping or by any information storage retrieval system without the written permission of the publisher except in the case of brief quotations embodied in critical articles and reviews.

WestBow Press books may be ordered through booksellers or by contacting:

WestBow Press
A Division of Thomas Nelson
1663 Liberty Drive
Bloomington, IN 47403
www.westbowpress.com
1-(866) 928-1240

Because of the dynamic nature of the Internet, any web addresses or links contained in this book may have changed since publication and may no longer be valid. The views expressed in this work are solely those of the author and do not necessarily reflect the views of the publisher, and the publisher hereby disclaims any responsibility for them.

Scripture quotations are from The Holy Bible, English Standard Version (ESV) copyright 2001 by Crossway, a publishing ministry of Good News Publishers. Used by permission. All rights reserved.

Any people depicted in stock imagery provided by Thinkstock are models, and such images are being used for illustrative purposes only.

Certain stock imagery © Thinkstock.

ISBN: 978-1-4497-7118-8 (sc)
ISBN: 978-1-4497-7119-5 (e)
ISBN: 978-1-4497-7120-1 (hc)

Library of Congress Control Number: 2012918948

Printed in the United States of America

WestBow Press rev. date: 11/28/2012

"We Wish to See Jesus" is a one year trip taken chronologically through the four Gospels from the circumstances surrounding Jesus' birth to His ascension. Each day presents a cogent thought of the Lord Jesus and those who followed Him. This book is intended to be used in conjunction with the Bible, not as a substitute for it.

Pastor Dennis Thomas had a life-changing encounter with Jesus Christ while in the Air Force at age 19 and has served in churches in South Dakota and Wisconsin for over 30 years.

For more information contact: onebibleteacher@q.com.

This book is dedicated to my three children
JOANNA, NAOMI & MATTHEW
and to their children,
and to their children's children

A special thanks to
Mike Hay (cover design)
Bob Osborn, Verda Pitzl and especially my good wife, Alta
for assisting in the preparation of this book

"WE WISH TO SEE JESUS"
Is intended to be a supplement to, not a substitute for
The Bible

Scripture quotations are from The Holy Bible, English Standard Version (ESV) copyright 2001 by Crossway, a publishing ministry of Good News Publishers. Used by permission. All rights reserved.

January 1
Read John 1:1-5

"In the beginning was the Word, and the Word was with God, and the Word was God. He was in the beginning with God" v. 1-2

Matthew begins his gospel with the genealogy of Jesus, linking Him to the Old Testament. Mark begins with Jesus actively serving in ministry. Luke begins with the historical events surrounding His birth. John begins in eternity past, before creation. His account of Christ's birth is in verse 14 — "The Word became flesh and dwelt among us".

If you had your DNA tested, it would be very difficult distinguish which part you got from your father and which part you got from your mother. You are a unique blend of both. The same is true with Jesus. He is a unique blend of God and man. It is an amazing truth to ponder. But we will never figure it out. Jesus is unique in all the universe —The God-man.

See also: Gen. 1:1, Col. 1:16-19, 1 Jn. 1:1-2

January 2
Read John 1:1-5

"All things were made through Him and without Him was not anything made that was made." v. 3

How much of the universe do we know about? Ken Taylor says, "We can only see as much of the universe as an amoeba can see of the ocean … All the glory the human eye can take in is comparable to the amoeba's single drop of water."

Scientists tell us that our galaxy, the Milky Way, is one-hundred thousand light years across and contains two-hundred million stars. One star, named Antares, has a diameter which would encompass the orbit of Mars! With all that said, our galaxy is one of an estimated one billion galaxies which cannot be seen by the naked eye!

To think that the One who created all the vastness of the universe still remembers that one amoeba swimming in a single drop of water is incredible! And He also remembers you! This great Creator took human form and came to this earth in the person of Jesus Christ.

See also: Gen. 1:1-31, Ps. 8:3-4, Heb. 1:1-4

January 3
Read Luke 1:1-4

"It seemed good to me also …to write an orderly account to you, most excellent Theophilus" v. 3

Luke was not one of the twelve disciples. Nor was he a Jew. He was a Gentile who became Paul's traveling companion (Col. 4:14). He got his information from 'eye witnesses and ministers of the word'(v. 2). He addresses his gospel, as well as the book of Acts, to a man named Theophilus.

Names in the Bible are very significant. Theophilus means "friend or lover of God". Except for Luke's mention of him we know nothing about him. But we can each make it our goal to be worthy of his name —"friend/lover of God." When we get to Heaven, we will meet both Luke and Theophilus. We can then thank Luke for writing this gospel and Theophilus for inspiring him!

See also: Acts 1:1-2, 2 Tim. 4:11

January 4
Read John 1:9-13

"But to all who did receive him, who believed in his name, he gave the right to become children of God" v. 12 [January Memory Verse]

Jesus is a gentleman. He will not force his way into our lives. He stands outside our heart's door and knocks. He will not tear the door down and barge in. We must open it to Him. When we do, we are transformed from the place of not knowing Him to the wonderful standing of being His children. This is a status even above angels. Angels are His creatures but they are never called His children as we are.

The action necessary on our part is what is here called "receiving" Him. Are the words of John 1:12 a reality in your heart today?

See also: 2 Cor. 5:17, 1 Jn.3:1-3, Rev. 3:20

January 5
Read John 1:9-13

"Who were born, not of blood nor of the will of the flesh nor of the will of man, but of God" v. 13

Christmas may be over-commercialized, but it certainly is not over-emphasized. It is so important that even our calendar is divided between BC and AD. If it were not for the birth and subsequent life of Jesus, all history would be different. The entire world would be barbaric today.

While the other gospels tell of Christ being born into the world, John tells of Him being born into our hearts and us being born into His kingdom. The hymn writer Philips Brooks put it this way:

O holy Child of Bethlehem, Descend to us we pray;

Cast out our sin and enter in; Be born in us today.

When this happens, any day of the year could be your personal Christmas!

See also: Is. 9:6, 1 Pet. 1:3

January 6
Read John 1:14-18

"And the Word became flesh and dwelt among us" v. 14

What is a word? It is the expression of a person; the basic communication of one person to another. But before words can be communicated there must be an intelligible pattern understood by both parties. If there are two different languages, the words need to be translated before they can be understood.

In our text today, "The Word became flesh". The heavenly word was translated into the earthly so we could understand what the God of Heaven is like.

In a very real sense today, the word needs to again become flesh and dwell among us. How will the world ever know about the God of Heaven unless the word becomes flesh in you and me?

Will you allow yourself to become a translation of the Word of God, so the world may be able to read your life and hear God speaking to them through you?

See also: 2 Cor. 3:2-3, Rev. 19:13

January 7
Read Matthew 1:1-17

"The book of the genealogy of Jesus Christ, the son of David, the Son of Abraham" v. 1

Mark was the first of the four gospels written. However, Matthew was placed first in sequence because it ties together the Old and New Testaments. Matthew wanted his readers to know that Jesus was the fulfillment of the promises of the Old Testament. God gave covenants to both Abraham and David. That is why their names are in verse one. In about 2000 BC, Abraham was promised a land and a people. In about 1000 BC, David was promised a kingdom that would last forever. Both of these covenants are fulfilled in Christ.

The first time I read the book of Matthew, I wondered why the writer "wasted" his time writing a long genealogy. Now I read it and marvel at how God kept his promise generation after generation after generation! Even in God's chosen family, there was turmoil and evil. In spite of that, God was faithful!

Going through the twists and turns of this life, God will be faithful to you as well. His promises will be fulfilled. We will end up safely on Heaven's eternal shore. You can count on it!

See also: Gen. 12:1-3, Deut. 7:9, 2 Sam. 7:12-13, Ps. 145:13

January 8
Read Matthew 1:1-16

"Salmon, the father of Boaz by Rahab" v. 5

Rahab of Jericho is one of five women named in Jesus' genealogy. The odds that she would be in the 'Who's Who?' column of Jewish history were highly unlikely. She was a gentile. She was a woman. She was a prostitute. If that were not enough, she lived in a city that God had destined for complete destruction. These obstacles were overcome by one thing — faith!

We read in Hebrews 11:31, "By faith, Rahab the prostitute did not perish with those who were disobedient, because she had given a friendly welcome to the spies." Not only was her life spared, but she also became the progenitor to the Lord Jesus Christ! Those of us who are saved because of Him, owe at least part of our eternal blessing to Rahab!

Is there any life that is beyond the grace of God? Faith trumps every obstacle. Just ask Rahab!

See also: Josh. 6:22-25, Js. 2:25

January 9
Read Luke 1:5-17

"But the angel said to him, 'Do not be afraid, Zachariah, for your prayer has been heard, and your wife Elizabeth will bear you a son, and you shall call his name John'" v. 13

John's birth is what I call a "providential childhood." That is when something unique occurs in the birth or early life of a child which shows God's fingerprints on that life. Moses and Samuel were also providential children. There are also providential children today. Perhaps you have heard of someone who survived an abortion or overcame severe problems as an infant.

When I was six weeks old, I had a pyloric tumor which made it impossible for me to swallow food. Literally starving to death, I weighed less than when I was born. Dr. Olson told my mother I had three days to live. She put me into the hands of God and a surgeon. I underwent a very serious operation, and guess what — I lived to tell about it! Whereas a tiny and forgotten headstone in a cemetery could have been the only thing that remained of my short life, instead, today, some 60 years later, you are reading a book I wrote about Jesus. Isn't that providential?!

PS Thanks for praying, Mom!

See also: Ex. 2:1-10, 1 Sam. 1:12-20, Mal. 4:5-6

January 10
Read Luke 1:5-17

"He will be great before the Lord. And he must not drink wine or strong drink, and he will be filled with the Holy Spirit" v. 15

In Gabriel's message to Zechariah about his son, between "He will be great before the Lord", and "He will be filled with the Holy Spirit" are the words, "He must not drink wine or strong drink". This was one of the requirements of the forerunner of the Savior.

Perhaps others in Israel were permitted to drink. But this was not permitted for the one who was going to introduce the Christ.

Christ is coming again. We are forerunners of His second coming. We have the special task of preparing souls for His return. Knowing this, let us also sanctify ourselves for the task. This may even mean abstaining from alcohol in every form.

See also: Prov. 20:1, Prov. 23:29-35, Eph 5:18

January 11
Read Luke 1:67-79

"(The Lord God of Israel) has raised up a horn of salvation for us in the house of His servant David" v. 69

Salvation: God thought it
                Jesus bought it
                The Spirit brought it
                The Bible taught it
                The church caught it
                And I got it!   Amen!   (Copied)

See also: Ps. 37:39, Ps. 85:9, Acts 4:12, Rom. 1:16, Rev. 7:10

January 12
Read Matthew 1: 18-25

"She will bear a son, and you shall call His name Jesus, for He will save His people from their sins" v. 21

    Our biggest problem is our sin. Our greatest need is for a Savior. But salvation goes deeper than most people think. God has a three-fold solution to our sin problem:
1. We have been saved from sin's <u>penalty</u> because of the finished work of Christ on our behalf.
2. We are being saved from sin's <u>power</u> as we live in daily dependence on Him through the power of the Holy Spirit.
3. We will be saved from sin's <u>presence</u> when we leave this world and enter into our heavenly home.

    Sin's effects run deep, even to the very core of our being. But thank God that His provisions run even deeper!

See also: Ps. 103:12, Rom. 6:14, 1 Jn. 1:9

January 13
Read Matthew 1:18-25

"And they shall call his name Immanuel" (which means, God with us)" v. 23

In the minds of many people, the major thought of Christmas is <u>presents</u>. But the real thought of Christmas should be <u>Presence</u> —God's presence!

We should not think of God's presence on earth as being only those few years when Jesus walked the earth. By his Spirit, He is still present with us today — right now!

The first chapter of Matthew says, "God with us". The last chapter says, "Behold, I am with you always, to the end of the age" (Mt. 28:20). Though He is not physically here, He is with us by His Spirit. He is your Emmanuel right here, right now! Believe it. Live it. Then others will see His presence in you!

See also: Ps. 139:7-12, 2 Cor. 1:22, 1 Jn. 4:13

January 14
Read Luke 2:1-7

"In those days a decree went out from Caesar Augustus that all the world should be registered" v. 1

Caesar Augustus was a heathen potentate sitting in Rome who had no regard for the living God and knew nothing of the Jewish holy writings or their hope of a Messiah. His interests were power and money. He made a decree for one reason—taxation. He did not know nor care that his decree would cause great distress on a peasant girl by forcing her to go to a small hamlet he had never heard of named Bethlehem. There, she gave birth to a son in fulfillment of a prophecy that was written some seven-hundred years earlier!

How great is the foreknowledge and providence of our God! He could direct the decisions and timing of a selfish heathen king to bring about his plan to have Mary in Bethlehem on the very day of Christ's birth! Even a heathen king is used to fulfill God's will and word!

And who is in charge today? Is it people in high office? No. It is our God! What a comfort in a time of distress and uncertainty!

See also: Jer. 29:11, Mic. 5:2, Gal. 4:4, 1 Pet. 1:2

January 15
Read Luke 2:1-7

"And she gave birth to her firstborn son and wrapped Him is swaddling cloths and laid Him in a manger, because there was no place for them in the inn" v. 7

On a December day I was talking with some elementary school kids about the Christmas story. I asked them what animals were at the stable. They started giving the usual list. Then one kid said, "Mice." In all my years of pondering the Christmas story I had never thought of mice being at the stable, but that kid was probably right!

Author Jill Richardson writes, "Christmas is a squalling newborn in a dirty feeding trough. It is unwashed shepherds smelling of sheep. It is a frightened teen mother too poor to reserve a room and too shocking to stay with relatives."

None of us have yet had a perfect Christmas. Neither was the first one. But in the midst of all kinds of hard circumstances we have been given the gift of the Christ! How wonderful!

See also: Is. 9:6-7, 2 Cor. 9:15

January 16
Read Luke 2:8-14

"The angel said to them, 'Fear not, for behold, I bring you good news of great joy that will be for all the people'" v. 10

There is a difference between good history and good news. History is something that happened in the past. News is something that is happening now. Sadly, many in the church today treat Christ's coming like history instead of news. However, when someone hears of the Savior coming to rescue fallen man and responds to it, it becomes good news — something that is happening right now!

When the One who was born in Bethlehem is born into our hearts, it is more than just good history. It truly is good news!
PS. It's also good theology!

See also: Is. 9:6-7, Rom. 1:16, 1 Pet. 1:3

January 17
Read Luke 2:8-14

"For unto you is born this day in the city of David a Savior, who is Christ the Lord" v. 11

    If our greatest need had been information, God would have sent an educator.

    If our greatest need had been technology, God would have sent a scientist.

    If our greatest need had been money, God would have sent an economist.

    If our greatest need had been pleasure, God would have sent an entertainer.

    But our greatest need was forgiveness. So God sent a Savior! (Copied)

See also: Is. 43:1, Titus 3:4-5, 1 Jn. 4:14

January 18
Read Luke 2:8-14

"Glory to God in the highest, and on earth peace among those with whom He is pleased" v. 14

    A little girl was asked to write an essay on Armistice Day. She wrote: "Armistice Day was November 11, 1918, and since then we have had two minutes of peace every year."

    A poll of college students revealed that personal peace is one of the greatest desires of this generation. Although the world seeks peace, Ezekiel 7:25 says, "When anguish comes, they will seek peace, but there shall be none."

    The pledge made by the angel was not for world peace (at least not at this time), but for peace in the hearts of those who please God. Only those who have the <u>God of peace</u> can have the <u>peace of God</u>.

See also: Num. 6:24-26, Ps. 29:11, Phil. 4:6-7, Phil. 4:9

January 19
Read Luke 2:15-20

"And when they saw it, they made known the saying that had been told them concerning this child" v. 17

The major emphasis of the shepherd's message was not a story of seeing a vision, or seeing angels, or hearing them speak, but of "this child"—Jesus. The most important thing is to keep the most important thing the most important thing. People sometimes get sidetracked by an experience or a feeling, when the emphasis needs to be on Jesus. People need to be pointed to Him, not to our experience. He is the one who changes hearts and lives, not my experience.

See also: Rom. 1:8, 1 Cor. 15:3-4, 1 Thess. 1:8

January 20
Read Luke 2:22-32

"For my eyes have seen Your salvation that You have prepared in the presence of all peoples" v. 30-31

D L Moody was a great evangelist who lived in the late 1800's. During his lifetime, he spoke to literally millions of people — and without a microphone! When he died, the following words were found written on the inside cover of his Bible:

Salvation is:

Justification:	A change of standing before God
Regeneration:	A change of nature from God
God Repentance:	A change of mind about God
God Conversion:	A change of life for God
God Adoption:	A change of family in God
God Sanctification:	A change of service to God
God Glorification:	A change of place with God

When Simeon was in the temple and said, "My eyes have seen your salvation", he was looking at Jesus. Jesus is the salvation of God and all the wonderful things that go with it!

See also: Ps. 37:39, Acts 13:47, Heb. 2:3, Rev. 7:10

January 21
Read Luke 2:36-38
"There was a prophetess, Anna...She was advanced in years..." v. 36

Our society places a great emphasis on natural beauty and youth. But have you ever noticed the beauty of an elderly person? Often I look at certain older people with grey hair and wrinkles and see a godly beauty that can never be found in younger people. Although the flower of youth has long faded, God has developed a beauty of character that only comes from years of walking with Him. Time has produced an imperishable quality that will never fade. Anna was one of those people. She never retired from serving her God.

Let us practice a lifestyle of daily walking with our Savior, so when our natural beauty fades, God's eternal beauty may be displayed.

See also: Prov. 31:10-31, Col. 3:10, 1 Pet. 3:4

January 22
Read Matthew 2:1-6
"Behold, wise men from the east came to Jerusalem, saying, 'Where is He who has been born king of the Jews? For we saw His star when it rose and have come to worship Him'" v. 1-2

Matthew presents Jesus as king; Mark presents Him as servant; Luke presents Him as man; John presents Him as God. Revelation 4:7 represents these same four aspects as the lion, ox, man and eagle in the heavenly realm.

As you read Matthew, take special note of the words 'King' and 'kingdom', which is the key word of the book. Take note also of how this King fulfills Old Testament prophecies.

When we became Christians, we entered His Kingdom. As His subjects, we need to realize daily that if we are in His kingdom we need to submit to the King and obey His every word!

See also: Ps. 45:6, Ps. 145:13, Dan. 7:14, Rev. 11:15, Rev. 19:16

January 23
Read Matthew 2:1-6

"They assembled all the chief priests and scribes of the people, and inquired of them where the Christ was to be born" v. 4

In chapter two of Matthew's gospel, we see three different groups — The Magi, Herod, and the Jewish leaders. The Magi, although they most likely did not have access to the Holy Writings, came hundreds of miles, with extreme sacrifice and risk, to find the Christ. But the priests, who were the custodians of the Scriptures, would not go just a few miles to investigate their fulfillment.

While the Magi were true-believers, Herod was an unbeliever and the priests were make-believers. They were too apathetic to take one step of faith in response to their own sacred writings. Their indifference to God's word turned to hatred some thirty years later when they had the Christ crucified.

Which would best describe your life — that of a true-believer, or an unbeliever, or a make-believer?
PS. There are also pre-believers whom you and I have not yet introduced to the Savior!

See also: Heb. 11:6, Js. 2:18,26

January 24
Read Matthew 2:1-6

"And you, O Bethlehem, in the land of Judah, are by no means least among the rulers of Judah; for from you shall come a ruler who will shepherd My people Israel" v. 6

Where did God choose to have the Savior born? Was it Rome, the political capital of the world which sent its armies everywhere in the civilized world? No. Or in Athens where culture and learning influenced the world for centuries? No. How about Jerusalem, where the temple to the one true God was built? No again. God chose Bethlehem, a town of only a few hundred people. If it were not for the birth of our Savior there, we would have never heard of Bethlehem.

Most people live in obscure places — places that only a few people even know exist. But that doesn't mean it is insignificant to God. It seems that God does His best work in obscure places with insignificant people. Your community is important to God. (It really is!) Just look around you. I bet you can see God at work!

See also: Ps. 8:3-4, 1 Cor. 1:26-29

January 25
Read Matthew 2:16-18

"Then was fulfilled what was spoken by the prophet…" v. 17

Just because something is predicted by God does not mean it is His will. God is not the author of evil. He is not responsible for what Herod did. Nor is He responsible for what Adam and Eve did in the garden — nor for what you or I do.

The prophecy of children being killed in Bethlehem was not based on God's sovereign will but on His foreknowledge. Herod was not a helpless puppet. He had a free will. And acting out of his free will, he will give account of his actions on the Day of Judgment.

There is a place in every human heart that even God will not enter without permission. He never takes our free will away from us. He wants us to surrender it freely to Him.

See also: Gen. 2:16-17, Rev. 22:17

January 26
Read Luke 2:41-50

"Supposing Him to be in the group, they went a day's journey" v. 44

From what is known about the culture of Jesus' day, people would travel in caravans for safety. Men would be in one group while women and children were in another group. Jesus at age twelve could have been in either group. Therefore, both Joseph and Mary thought He was in the other's group.

How many of us are like Joseph and Mary, presuming Jesus is with us and entering into our plans and activities, but never making a conscious effort to be sure of His presence? If it seems that He is not with us, it may be because we have rushed ahead of Him without considering His will and plan for us. If He seems far away, it is not because He has moved away from us, but because we have moved away from Him!

Joseph and Mary returned to the place where they had last seen Jesus. And there they found Him! What a lesson for Christians who often stray like wandering sheep, not necessarily doing evil things but simply making decisions and entering into activities without Christ.

See also: Ex. 33:14, Josh. 9:14

January 27
Read Luke 2:51-52

"And Jesus increased in wisdom and in stature and in favor with God and man" v. 52

Jesus grew to become the world's only completely mature man. To mature is to become more like Jesus. Luke 2:52 tells us that He matured in four ways: In wisdom — mentally; In stature — physically; In favor with God —spiritually; In favor with man —socially.

Mentally, His every thought was under the control of the Holy Spirit. Physically, He had no over-indulgence of any kind. Spiritually, He was completely in harmony with the Heavenly Father. Socially, He had no animosity toward any person on earth.

God's grand design for us is to make us more like Jesus. In this world right now there is no such thing as a mature person. We may be maturing, but none of us are mature. Let us press on to become more like Jesus.

See also: Eph. 4:13, 2 Pet. 3:18

January 28
Read Luke 2:51-52

"And Jesus increased in ... favor with God" v. 52

Luke 2:40 (in most translations) says God's grace was upon Jesus. In verse 52, it says God's favor was upon Him. There is a difference between the grace of God and the favor of God. Grace comes when we trust God. His favor comes when He can trust us. Grace is based on His character. Favor is based on our character. Grace comes because He is faithful. But His favor comes when we are faithful.

It is wonderful to know the grace of God. But let us go on to maturity and enter into His favor. Is God pleased with you? Is He happy with you? Is His smile upon you? Let us mature to the point where we can to be found in His favor.

When speaking of us, may His words be, "You are my beloved (child), with you I am well pleased" (Mt. 3:17).

See also: Col. 1:10, Col. 1:28, 1 Thess. 5:23

January 29
Read John 1:6-8

"There was a man sent from God, whose name was John. He came as a witness to bear witness about the light " v. 6

John the Baptist is described as, "A man (with <u>human limitations</u>) sent from God (with <u>divine authorization</u>) whose name was John (of <u>personal recognition</u>) who came to bear witness (a <u>special occupation</u>) about the light" (v. 6-7).

Like John, we are also limited by human weakness. But God knows us personally and calls us individually to the same special task of bearing witness to the light. Because of this, we can put our own name in our Bible beside John's name.

Bearing witness to the light is to be the primary occupation of every Christian in the world.

See also: Is. 6:8-9, Acts 1:8, 1 Jn. 1:5-7

January 30
Read Mark 1:4-8

"And all the country of Judea and all Jerusalem were going out to him and were being baptized by him in the river Jordan, confessing their sins" v. 5

When our son was about five years old he would occasionally get himself into interpersonal problems with others. One day, after offending a little friend, he was asked to say he was sorry. His response in a slow monotone voice was, "I can't say that word."

When we offend someone, we often make the excuse that our vocabulary is too limited to say we are sorry. We try to justify our own sin by condemning someone else. But confession is God's way of restoring a relationship that was broken.

Just imagine how many people are in the world who have offended their Creator, yet sit stubbornly muttering, "I can't say that word". But with John the Baptist, people said it by the thousands! Imagine what would happen today if great numbers would come and say 'I am sorry' before God! Let's pray that happens again!

See also: Is. 55:7, Acts 3:19, Acts 26:20

January 31
Read John 1:19-28

"(John) said, 'I am the voice of one crying out in the wilderness, 'Make straight the way of the Lord'" v. 23

The coming of The Christ demanded that there be a herald to announce His arrival. People needed to be prepared for His coming. That was John's special mission. And now we are getting close to His second coming. If it was necessary for someone to announce His first coming, how much more important is it that His return be announced. I believe that to prepare the world for His coming again, God will raise up not the 'voice of one', but the voice of hundreds! No, thousands! No, millions!

Whether we are alive or not when Jesus returns, each of us are going to meet Him and give account to Him. In John's generation, he was the voice of one. In my generation, I want to be the voice of another. If you would be the voice of still another, we will soon have an entire chorus of people saying, "Make straight the way of the Lord". Then, as far as we are concerned, no one would have an excuse for not being ready for His return.

See also: Mal. 4:5-6, Acts 4:20, Rom. 1:15, Rom. 10:14-15

February 1
Read Luke 3:10-14

"The crowds asked him, 'What then shall we do?'" v. 10

John's purpose in respect to preparing for the Christ was to preach repentance. Repentance means a change of mind which results in a change of lifestyle.

In response to John's preaching, three different groups (The crowds, v. 10 / Tax collectors, v. 12 / Soldiers, v. 14) asked the same question — "What shall we do?" John's answer to all three groups was the same — Change your mind about money. Change your thoughts from a temporal value system to an eternal value system. Value people more than things.

Money cannot buy our way into Heaven. But it can certainly prevent us from getting there. John's admonition was to get temporal treasures in the right perspective so we can receive the eternal treasures.

"Bear fruit in keeping with repentance." (v. 8). Have you done this with respect to money?

See also: Eccl. 5:10, 1 Tim. 6:6-10

February 2
Read Luke 4:1-13

"And Jesus, full of the Holy Spirit returned from the Jordan and was lead by the Spirit in the wilderness for forty days, being tempted by the devil" v. 1-2

Isaiah 14:12-15 and Ezekiel 28:11-17 tell us that Satan (also known as Lucifer) was an anointed angel before he rebelled against his Creator. (See Isaiah 14:13-14 for the 'I will's' of Satan.) He has great power, but is nowhere near as powerful as the omnipotent God. He is a creature while God is the Creator — an astronomical difference.

From our vantage point, it may appear that the power of God and the power of Satan are nearly equal. But Satan will be forever destroyed by the breath of Christ's mouth. He is destined to be banished forever and ever in the Lake of Fire (Rev. 20:7-10).

See also: 2 Cor. 11:13-15, 2 Thess. 2:8, 1 Pet. 5:8, Rev. 12:10-11

February 3
Read Mark 1:9-13

"And He was in the wilderness forty days, being tempted by Satan" v. 13

Among the descriptions of Satan in the Bible, three stand out in my mind:
1. An angel of light (2 Corinthians 11:14),
2. A roaring lion (1 Peter 5:8),
3. The accuser of the brothers (Revelation 12:10).

It is interesting how the devil uses people in each of these situations! Reading these verses in context will help you be equipped to overcome him. Please also be encouraged in knowing that, "He who is in you is greater than he who is in the world" (1 John 4:4). In the plan of God, Satan is already defeated. Amen!

See also: 2 Cor. 2:11, 2 Cor. 11:13-15, 1 Pet. 5:8-9, Rev. 12:7-11

February 4
Read Matthew 4:1-11

"It is written, 'Man shall not live by bread alone, but by every word that comes from the mouth of God'" v. 4

The first thing Satan did in the Garden of Eden was to challenge what God had said. And he is still doing that today. If we stand against him with our own arguments and reasonings, the result will be the same as that of Adam and Eve.

Each time Jesus resisted the devil, He did it the same way — by quoting Scripture. He had it committed to memory, which we also need to do, so we can stand when attacks come.

The only weapon with which we can stand against the attacks of the evil one is the Word of God. It is called 'The sword of the Spirit'! It will prevail. It is essential that we hide it in our hearts, so it can be used at the necessary time.

<u>Warning</u>: Please be certain that you are on the handle end and not the blade end of God's Sword!

See also: Ps. 119:11, Eph. 6:17, Heb. 4:12, Rev. 2:16

February 5
Read John 1:29-34

"Behold, the Lamb of God, who takes away the sin of the world!" v. 29

No one can come into the presence of God without a sacrifice that God can accept. In Genesis chapter four, Abel came with an acceptable offering (a lamb slain). But Cain's offering (the fruit of the ground) was not accepted. As the Old Testament continues, the priests brought a lamb without blemish and sacrificed it on the altar every year. This was done by faith, looking forward to Christ, the Lamb of God who would take away the sin of the world.

With what sacrifice shall we approach God? Some are trying to come before Him with the offering of self-righteousness or good works. If that were sufficient, then Christ's sacrifice is worthless. The sacrifice of Jesus, the Lamb of God, is the only offering God can accept.

See also: Gen. 4:1-7, Ex. 12:13-23, Heb. 9:22, Rev. 5:5-6

February 6
Read John 1:29-34

"And I have seen and have borne witness that this is the Son of God" v. 34

Jesus is the only link between God and man. The first chapter of John gives three pictures of how Jesus, the 'God-man' links us to our heavenly Father.

> v. 1-2 — As the Word of God who <u>reveals</u> God to man
>
> v. 29 — As the Lamb of God who <u>redeems</u> man to God
>
> v. 34 — As the Son of God who <u>reigns</u> as God over man

See also: 1 Cor. 8:5-6, 1 Tim. 2:5-6

February 7
Read John 1:35-42

"(John) looked at Jesus as He walked by and said, 'Behold the Lamb of God!'" v. 36

A missionary to Taiwan shared with us a one word sermon taken from the Chinese language. The word "righteous" written in Chinese is made up of two characters (word symbols). The top character is their word for lamb. The bottom character means 'me' or 'myself'. Therefore 'righteousness' in Chinese is a lamb over me.

Jesus is called the Lamb of God. How can I be righteous in the eyes of God? By placing myself under the Lamb. I am so happy for the day I did just that. Have you?

See also: Rom. 6:17, Rom. 10:4, Phil. 3:9

February 8
Read John 1:35-42

"The two disciples heard (John) say this, and they followed Jesus" v. 37

Here is another beautiful outline taken directly from John chapter one:

V. 19-28 —John only
V. 29-34 — John and Jesus
V. 35-42 — Jesus and John
V. 43-50 —Jesus only

John's disciples became disciples of Jesus. Christian leaders must make special effort to see that those who come to them also become followers of Jesus. John's words in John 3:30 need to be true of all of us —'He must increase, but I must decrease.'

See also: Acts 6:7, Acts 20:30

February 9
Read John 1:35-42

"He first found his own brother…He brought him to Jesus." v. 41, 42

The first question God asks man is "Where are you?" (Genesis 3:9). The second question is, "Where is…your brother?" (Genesis 4:9).

We see Andrew three times in the book of John (1:35-42, 6:8-11, 12:20-22). Each time he is bringing someone to Jesus. We don't read that he ever stood before a large crowd or made a public speech. He simply brought people one-by-one to Jesus. Thus, he was fulfilling his obligation to his fellow man by answering the question, 'Where is your brother?' He had the gift of personal evangelism.

Imagine the joy of standing in Heaven and seeing someone you personally brought to the Savior! Is there someone to whom God would have you say, "I have found the Messiah"? (v. 41)

See also: Rom. 1:15, 2 Tim. 4:5

February 10
Read John 1:35-42

"Jesus looked at him and said, 'So you are Simon, son of John? You shall be called Cephas.'" v. 42

God loves you just as you are—but too much to leave you that way! Every life our Lord touched He changed! His first words to Peter were, "You are... You shall be..."

If we look at people through natural eyes, we will never get beyond, "You are Simon (unsettled shifting sand)". But if we look at them through Christ's eyes, we can say, "You shall be called Cephas (a solid secure rock).

Instead of looking at people as they are, let's begin looking at them as they can be by the grace of God. Then let us begin working in harmony with God to bring those changes about.

See also: 1 Sam. 16:7, I Tim. 1:13-16

February 11
Read John 1:43-51

"Jesus answered him, 'Before Philip called you, when you were under the fig tree, I saw you'" v. 48

Wherever you were yesterday, whatever you did, God saw you.

When our grandson was small, he tried to come to terms with the fact that God saw him no matter where he was. First he hid under the table so God wouldn't see him. Realizing that wasn't working, he ran and found a blanket to squirm under. Finally he just gave up and tried to make peace with the fact that God always sees him.

Often knowledge of God's all-seeing eye gives us great peace. At other times, it may give us discomfort, knowing that we are accountable to Him. Either way, the truth of an all-knowing, all-seeing God is a healthy thought. The more we realize His <u>omniscience</u> (all knowledge) and His <u>omnipresence</u> (everywhere present) the better off we are.

As with Nathanael, God saw you and what you did this morning. May He be able to see 'no deceit' (v. 47) in you as well.
PS. It is encouraging also that we realize His <u>omnipotence</u> (all power).

See also: Ps. 139:1-12, Heb. 4:13, Rev. 6:16

February 12
Read John 2:1-11

"His mother said to the servants, 'Do whatever He tells you'" v. 5

There are four wills vying for supremacy in every person's life: his own will, the will of other people, the will of Satan, and the will of God. Which one we yield to will determine our destiny.

Jesus' mother Mary made two profound statements pertaining to following the will of God. The first was in Luke 1:38 after the angel Gabriel spoke to her, when she said, "Behold, I am the servant of the Lord; let it be done to me according to your word". The second is here — "Do whatever He tells you".

What a joyous thing it will be on the day we meet Jesus and see the wondrous things God has done because we did His will and not our own!

See also: Rom. 12:2, Eph. 5:17, Phil. 2:13, 1 Thess. 5:16-18

February 13
Read John 2:1-11

"Jesus said to the servants, 'Fill the jars with water'. And they filled them to the brim" v. 7

When the servants were told to fill the water jars, "they filled them to the brim." They did not do a half-way job. The jars were as full as they could be.

When I was in Alaska, I had opportunity to see some dogsled races. I was very impressed with the zeal and vigor of the Huskies as they pulled with pure determination. Just watching them pull the sleds produced admiration in the spectators. The driver's biggest concern was that they did not hurt themselves in their zeal. A cut foot that could cause permanent damage would not stop those enthusiastic animals (or should I say athletes?).

God expects us to do His work with diligence. If He has called us to a task, we should do it with all the ability He has given us.

See also: Rom. 12:11, Col. 3:23

February 14
Read John 2:1-11

"This, the first of His signs, Jesus did at Cana in Galilee, and manifested His glory. And His disciples believed in Him." v. 11

What is a sign? It is a miracle which points to the supernatural power of God; an illustration of a spiritual truth. Throughout his gospel, John speaks of signs.

What is the significance of Jesus' first sign — the turning of water into wine? It is an illustration of being born again, which is spoken of in the next chapter. The plain ordinary water of our lives is transformed into the richest beverage in the world. Our temporal lives are transformed into something eternal! This is "the beginning of signs" which Jesus wants to perform in our lives.

Are you born again? (Jn. 3:1-12) Has the water of your life been changed into wine? This, being the first sign, is the first thing God wants to do in your life.

Let Him take your plain, ordinary life and transform it into something beautiful. When your friends see the change, they also will "believe in Him"!

See also: Is. 43:18-19, 2 Cor. 5:17

February 15
Read John 2:1-11

"This, the first of His signs, Jesus did in Cana in Galilee, and manifested His glory. And His disciples believed in Him" v. 11

What is a disciple? If we are commanded to make disciples, we certainly should first know what a disciple is. And what better person could we ask than John, 'the disciple that Jesus loved'? (John 13:23, 19:26, 20:2, 21:7, 21:20). In his Gospel, he gives five marks of a disciple:

Jn. 2:11	A disciple believes
Jn. 8:31	A disciple abides in His Word
Jn. 13:35	A disciple loves
Jn. 15:8	A disciple bears fruit
Jn. 21:24	A disciple bears witness

Question: Are you a disciple? Which of the above traits do you need to work on to be a better disciple?

See also: Acts 11:26, Acts 13:52, Acts 14:22

February 16
Read John 2:13-17

"And making whip of cords, He drove them all out of the temple." v. 15

A temple is the dwelling place of God. Today there is no temple of wood or stone. God lives in the temple of our hearts. I Corinthians 3:16 says, "Do you not know that you are God's temple and that God's Spirit dwells in you?"

Jesus found it necessary to cleanse His temple in Jerusalem. At times, if we allow things into our lives which desecrate the temple of our bodies, He may find it necessary to purify us as well. And that isn't a pleasant experience! How much better it would be if we would cleanse ourselves.

See also: Ps. 51:2, 10, 1 Cor. 6:19-20, 2 Tim. 2:21, Heb. 12:5-11

February 17
Read John 3:1-8

"Jesus answered him, 'Truly, truly, I say to you, unless one is born again he cannot see the kingdom of God'" v. 3

Nicodemus had many advantages. He was a Jew. He was a Pharisee. He was a teacher. He knew the Holy Scriptures. But with all of these advantages he was still outside of the Kingdom of God.

Being born again is not revising or improving the old life. Jesus didn't offer Nicodemus a self-improvement class. He said Nicodemus had to go all the way back to the beginning and start over. This new start is called being born again, or born anew, or born from above, or born of the Spirit. It is not a reformation but a transformation.

My old Adam nature has nothing that God can accept. We need to leave it behind and start over. Have you come to the point of leaving your old life behind and starting a new life where you are born from above?

See also: Is. 64:6, Jer. 17:9, Rom. 7:18, Gal. 6:15

February 18
Read John 3:1-13

"Do not marvel that I said to you, 'You must be born again'" v. 7

Are you tired of who you are? Do you wish you could be someone different? The answer is not found in moving to a new house, getting a new job, or finding a new mate. The answer is found in getting a new heart. And that is exactly what God wants to do with each one of us!

The Great Physician specializes in heart transplants. In Ezekiel 36:26, God says, "I will give you a new heart, and a new spirit I will put within you". God wants to give us a heart transplant! He has issued a recall on all broken and sinful hearts. All we need to do is come to Him with our need. When we do, everything is different. That is not because the world around us changes, but a change takes place from within. That is what Jesus called being "born again"!

See also: Ezek. 36:25-27, 1 Pet. 1:3

February 19
Read John 3:14-18

"For God so loved the world that He gave His only Son" v. 16

Don Richardson was a missionary to the Sawi people in Irian Jaya. He looked for a way to communicate the Gospel to them. Then he discovered that all acts of kindness were viewed with suspicion except one. If a father would give his own son to his enemy to become part of their family, he could be trusted. This son was called the "peace child." Also, if anyone touched that child, he was brought into a friendly relationship with the father. Tribal wars ceased in one day if such an act were performed.

God gave His one and only Son. Reach out and touch Him and you will immediately be brought into a friendly relationship with the Father!
PS. The movie "Peace Child" was produced to show this Sawi practice. It would be worth your time to go on line and view it!

See also: Rom. 5:1, 2 Cor. 5:19

February 20
Read John 3:16-21

"For God so loved the world that He gave His only Son that whoever believes in Him should not perish but have eternal life" v. 16 [February Memory Verse]

It has been said that you can give without loving, but you cannot love without giving. John 3:16 tells us who the recipients of God's love are: 1. The world, which encompasses everyone, and 2. "Whoever," which speaks of the individual.

You may not be recognized as being important or valuable in the eyes of the world. But in the eyes of God you are of immeasurable worth. You may consider yourself to be small and insignificant. But at least you are a "whoever." Therefore, you can say:

I am a whoever.

I am a whoever that God loves.

I am a whoever that believes in Jesus.

I am a whoever that has eternal life!

See also: 1 Cor. 1:26-29, 1 Jn. 4:10

February 21
Read John 3:31-36

"He who comes from above is above all" v. 31

All religions should be treated with equal value, right? Then let's hold them to the same standards. Did Buddha claim to have created the world? Did Muhammad die for your sins? Did Confucius rise from the dead? Have any of them ascended to Heaven? Are any of them going to return to rule the earth?

In reality there are only two religions in the world — the right one (centered in Jesus) and the wrong one (all the others). Jesus is in a category of His own. No one else can attain to His works or words. He is the One that all the world needs to look to for salvation. He is also the One to whom Buddha, Muhammad, Confucius, and every other mortal on earth will give account.

See also: Acts 4:12, Phil. 2:9-11

February 22
Read John 3:31-36

"Whoever believes in the Son has eternal life; whoever does not obey the Son shall not see life, but the wrath of God remains on him" v. 36

There are three kinds of death. The <u>first</u> is spiritual death. This occurred in the Garden of Eden when our first parents disobeyed God (Genesis 2:17). Each of us was born into this world in a state of spiritual deadness, separated from our Creator. We inherited this position from our first parents.

<u>Second</u>, there is physical death. This occurs when we die, and our body and soul separate. There is a 100% death rate for every generation.

<u>Third</u>, there is eternal death. This is the most severe of all. It will occur when God judges unrepentant sinners and eternally banishes them from His presence into outer darkness. Eternal death is also called "the second death" (Revelation 20:6).

God wants no one to experience eternal death. That is why Jesus came. "Whoever believes in the Son has eternal life." Amen

See also: Rom. 6:23, Rev. 20:14, Rev. 21:8

February 23
Read Mark 6:14-18

"John had been saying to Herod, 'It is not lawful for you to have your brother's wife'" v. 18

When a man and woman stand before both God and man and say, "For better, for worse; for richer, for poorer; in sickness and in health; from this day forth; until death do us part", that is exactly what God expects of them.

A man and wife were happily married until she began to suffer from brain deterioration. She required more and more care until finally she was reduced to life in bed. Then she lost control of her bodily functions. Such circumstances made it necessary for her husband to quit his job and dedicate total care to her. He stayed at her bedside until the day came when she left this world and he laid her in the arms of Jesus. His words at that point were, "I married her for better or worse, and things got worse." What a picture of devotion!

It is tragic in our day that the standards of Hollywood have a greater bearing on our relationships than the standards of God. Nevertheless, let us who name the name of Christ maintain His ideal.

See also: Gen. 2:24, Eph. 5:22-33, Heb. 13:4

February 24
Read John 4:1-18

"Whoever drinks of the water that I will give him will never be thirsty again. The water that I will give him will become in him a spring of water welling up to eternal life." v. 14

The Samaritan woman's first husband did not meet her needs. Neither did her second. Nor her third. Nor her fourth. Nor her fifth! There is a vacuum in the human heart that can only be met by Christ. But how many of us are like this woman, expecting others to meet the needs that only Jesus can meet?

When we come to Christ, we not only find ourselves satisfied, but we also become "a spring of water" which others can come to and find the Christ, as well.

Someone thirsting for God may come to your well today to find living water. May that person be fully satisfied.

See also: Is. 55:1, 1 Jn. 5:11-13, Rev. 21:6

February 25
Read John 4:19-26

"The hour is coming, and is now here when the true worshipers will worship the Father in spirit and truth, for the Father is seeking such people to worship him." v. 23

Our worship of God must be in spirit (a <u>right heart</u>) and in truth (a <u>right head</u>). We will never go astray if we keep these two things in balance.

Many people think that when they gather together to worship, the pastor and musicians are the performers and the congregation is the audience. In reality, the people up front are simply prompters to worship. The congregation is the performers and God is the audience. As we gather to worship in spirit and truth, let us not forget the most important One attending the service! He has promised that when we gather in His name, that He Himself is in our midst (Mt. 18:20).

See also: Ps. 22:3, Heb. 10:19-25

February 26
Read John 4:27-30

"Come, see a man who told me all that I ever did. Can this be the Christ?" v. 29

The Samarian woman's concept of who Jesus is grew from Him being "a Jew" (v. 9), to "a prophet" (v. 19), to "the Christ" (v. 29). When we talk to others about Jesus, we feel that we have failed unless we have "led them to Christ." But if we bring them to a place of greater understanding of who He is, we have been successful. In the future, other faithful witnesses can then build on what we have said, even if they don't know us or what we have said. God is faithful by His grace to bring people to Himself just as He was faithful to me and you.

See also: Job 42:5-6, Phil. 1:6

February 27
Read John 4:31-38

"Do you not say, 'There are yet four months, then comes the harvest'? Look, I tell you, lift up your eyes, and see that the fields are white for harvest" v. 35

How do you view people? Are they obstacles hindering your agenda or are they opportunities that God has put in your path to fulfill His agenda? To see people through the eyes of Jesus is very different than seeing them through your own eyes.

A "Divine Appointment" is defined as a time when the path of a searcher for Christ crosses the path of a servant of Christ. The timing of Jesus meeting the Samaritan woman was certainly divinely orchestrated. As a result, Jesus changed His schedule and stayed in Samaria two days (v. 40).

Even today, someone may come across your path that you were not expecting. Could this be a divine appointment!?

See also: Eccl. 3:1-8, 2 Cor. 5:16, Rev. 14:15

February 28
Read John 4:39-42

"It is no longer because of what you said that we believe, for we have heard for ourselves, and we know that this is indeed the Savior of the world." v. 42

I am not discouraged about the status of mankind in the world, for I know that one hour in the light can dispel decades of darkness.

The people of Samaria came to Jesus because of the witness of a woman. But believing because of what someone else said is a second-hand faith. A personal encounter with Jesus Christ is necessary.

Why do you believe in Jesus? Is it because of what others have said? Do you hold to your faith simply because of what your parents have taught you? Or have you had a personal encounter with Him?

See also: Job 42:5, Is. 9:2, Acts 4:20, 1 Jn. 5:13, 1 Jn. 5:20

February 29
Read Matthew 4:12-17

"From that time Jesus began to preach, saying, 'Repent, for the kingdom of Heaven is at hand'" v. 17

Jesus' first public word was "Repent". Repentance is a forgotten word in our society. But it is absolutely essential if we are going to enter the Kingdom of Heaven. The gift of salvation is like a two-sided coin with repentance on one side and faith on the other. The two cannot be separated.

'Repent' means to change your mind; to be indeed sorry for the way you have lived; to take a spiritual U-turn. It also means to be sorry enough for what you have done to make a change. When we see our Lord as He truly is, repentance is our natural response.

See also: Job 42:5-6, Acts 2:37-38, 1 Thess. 1:9

March 1
Read Luke 5:1-11

"And Simon answered, 'Master, we toiled all night and took nothing! But at your word I will let down the nets'" v. 5

Sometimes God asks us to do something mundane or redundant. Our first impulse is like Peter's — "We've done that before and didn't get any results." Peter obeyed simply because his Lord told him to do it. The end result was a net-breaking, boat-sinking catch of fish! Isn't it amazing what a simple act of obedience can produce!

Even if we don't see immediate results, obedience to God's word is never fruitless. Maybe He is working behind the scenes doing something that we won't see until eternity. Let's obey God even in the little things and leave the results to Him.

See also: Deut. 11:13-14, Heb. 11:13

March 2
Read Matthew 4:18-22

"And He said to them, 'Follow Me and I will make you fishers of men'" v. 19

"Follow Me" is the essence of the Christian life. To be a leader of men we must first be followers of Jesus. But if we are going to follow Him, there must be some leaving on our part just as there was with the first disciples. First, they left their occupations. Second, they left their families. And it didn't take them long to leave, because twice in the passage, we read the word 'immediately'.

Establishing a relationship with Christ changes all other relationships. Any leaving, any forsaking is well worth it, for the excellency of serving Christ. If you forsake something or someone to follow Jesus, remember that He forsook Heaven for you.

See also: Gen. 12:1, Phil 2:7-11, Phil. 3:7-8

March 3
Read Matthew 4:18-22

"Immediately they left their nets and followed Him" v. 20

From 1804 through 1806 Lewis and Clark made their epic journey from St. Louis to the Pacific Ocean and back with their "Corps of Discovery." As they were portaging the Missouri river at what is now called Great Falls, Montana, Lewis wrote in his journal, "All have made up their minds to succeed in the expedition or perish in the attempt." What a resolve!

Christians are not on an expedition for a few months or a few years, but for a lifetime. Our destiny is not just crossing some mountains and following a river to the ocean, but Heaven itself! But we as disciples of Christ need to make a resolve similar to that of the Corps of Discovery. We will not stop. We will not turn back. We will reach our goal.

Are you up to the expedition?

See also: 2 Tim. 4:7-8, Rev. 7:13-14

March 4
Read Mark 1:40-45

"Moved with pity, he stretched out his hand and touched him" v. 41

The medical profession adheres to a very simple law. Anything that touches something unclean automatically becomes unclean. The pure is always defiled by the impure. It is a law of nature.

The ancient Israelites knew this law. Lepers were to keep separate from others. Under no circumstances would a healthy person touch a leper.

But Jesus, the clean, touched a leper, the unclean. The clean touched the unclean and the unclean became clean! The natural law was reversed. Oh, the wonderful power of God to reverse the law of nature!

The same principle is true in relationship to holiness. If the High and Holy One touches an unclean sinner's heart, that person becomes pure, becomes holy.

Are you impure, defiled, unholy? If you allow the Holy One to touch you, He will cleanse you. Let Him have that dirty part of your life. His touch will make it holy!

See also: 1 Cor. 6:9-11

March 5
Read Matthew 4:23-25

"They brought Him all the sick, those afflicted with various diseases and pains, those oppressed by demons, epileptics, and paralytics, and He healed them" v. 24

When our daughter was only a few months old, she contracted a virus that infants often get. In my concern for her, I said to myself, 'If I could, I would take that virus into my own body so she would not need to suffer so.' Naturally I couldn't do that. But in thinking about it, that is exactly what Jesus did for us.

Realizing that God was even more concerned for my daughter than I was, I began to pray. Within a day, the problem was gone. Thank the Lord!

Isaiah 53:5 says, "With His stripes we are healed." This means all kinds of healings —physical, emotional, spiritual. Let's approach Him in confidence with our needs, knowing that He is both willing and able to help us.

See also: Rom. 8:32, Heb. 4:16, 1 Pet. 2:24

March 6
Read Matthew 8:14-17

"This was to fulfill what was spoken by the prophet Isaiah: 'He took our illnesses and bore our diseases'" v. 17

If you want to know about fulfilled prophecies, Isaiah 53:4-6 is the place to start. Matthew 8:16-17 is the fulfillment of the healing aspect of that verse. But it is not just a 'one day long-long ago' fulfillment. This verse convinced me that healing is available for us today. It can still be fulfilled in us today.

Romans 8:32 says, "He who did not spare His own Son but gave Him up for us all, How will He not also with Him graciously give us all things?" One of those "all things" is physical healing. If He is able to take care of our sins, He is also able to also take care of our sicknesses.

God does not always do things the way we expect. But the promise of a fulfillment of this prophecy is available for us today — for me and for you!

See also: Is. 53:1-6, Js. 5:14-15

March 7
Read Mark 2:1-12

"And they came, bringing to Him a paralytic carried by four men" v. 3

Four nameless men carried their friend to Jesus. They put forth great effort to accomplish this goal. But their faith was rewarded. Their friend was healed!

There are times in every life when our circumstances get so bad that we can't get to Jesus on our own. That is when we need others around us to bring us to Jesus through prayer. Thank God for the faithful few who often remain unnamed, nevertheless do a wonderful work of bringing needy people one by one to Jesus in prayer. They have a vitally important role in the church.

As we think of the wonderful things God has done in our lives, let us pause and thank Him for the ones who faithfully brought us to Christ through prayer.

PS. Is there anyone around you that has a special need? Why don't you right now pick that person up and carry him to Jesus in prayer?

See also: Eph. 6:18-20, Js. 5:14-15

March 8
Read Mark 2:13-17

"(Jesus) said to him, 'Follow Me'. And he rose and followed Him" v. 16

A professor at a Bible college gave his students two blank sheets of paper for their final exam. He instructed them to spend the first half of the period writing all they could about the Holy Spirit, and the second half, writing about the devil. One student got so engrossed in the first half of the test that he completely forgot about the second half. When the period was over, he quickly wrote on the bottom of the page, "I spent so much time with the Holy Spirit that I forgot about the devil."

In our Scripture today, we read about Levi (Matthew) leaving his life's occupation to follow Jesus. No doubt he could have identified with that college student!

See also: Gal. 2:20, Phil. 1:21

March 9
Read Mark 3:1-6

"And He looked around at them with anger, grieved at their hardness of heart" v. 5

All truth needs to be balanced. We cannot emphasize one truth or doctrine at the expense or neglect of another. The Bible weaves truth together into a beautiful tapestry.

One of the fallacies of our day is the idea that Jesus never got angry. The thought that God is looking down and smiling at the human race might make us feel good but it is not fully accurate. Jesus was angry at the hypocrisy of His day. He is just as indignant with the sins of our day. And just as a day came when He judged past societies in His righteous anger, so that day is coming for America —and for each person individually.

Our hardness of heart pains His heart just as it did in Noah's generation (Genesis 6:5-6). His judgment for good or for bad awaits every nation and each individual.

See also: Gen. 6:5-6, Ps. 2:12, Rom. 1:18, 2 Cor. 5:10, Rev. 6:15-17

March 10
Read Mark 3:7-12

"A great crowd followed, from Galilee and Judea and Jerusalem and Idumea and from beyond the Jordan and from around Tyre and Sidon" v.8

Jesus drew quite a following! People from all over the region were drawn to Him—thousands! And is anything happening today? Are His followers only a small handful of souls?

I heard recently that around the world nearly 250,000 people per day make a commitment to Christ! That means nearly two million people per week! That is not just statistics. Every one of them is a real person. There is a quiet revolution going on around the globe — a spiritual revolution of souls coming one-by-one to Christ. Although the media isn't reporting it, God is raising up a people for Himself all over the world— today / right now —even from your home town. ' Maybe even you —today!

God hasn't given up on this world. Neither should we.

See also: Acts 2:47, 5:14, 6:7, 9:31, 11:24, 14:1, 16:5, Rev. 7:9

March 11
Read Luke 5:17-26

"That you may know that the Son of Man has authority on earth to forgive sins" v. 24

There are two realms mentioned in the Bible — the earthly realm and the heavenly realm. The first four letters of realm are 'real'. The heavenly realm is just as real as the earthly realm. When studying prophecy, the first question to ask is, 'Which realm are they talking about?'

Jesus, the Son of Man, forgives sins not in Heaven but on earth. Forgiveness is a present reality. We do not wait to leave this world to find out if our sins are forgiven. And notice when Jesus pronounced forgiveness on this man — 'when He saw their faith' (v. 20).

Jesus came to earth not to condemn but to forgive. It is the mission of the church to proclaim forgiveness to every person on earth.

See also: Acts 2:38-39, Eph. 1:7, Col. 1:14

March 12
Read Luke 5:27-32

"I have not come to call the righteous but sinners to repentance" v. 32

In 1742, John Wesley visited Newcastle, England and wrote: "So much drunkenness and swearing — even from the mouths of children — I have never witnessed before. Surely this place is ripe for Him who came not to call the righteous but sinners to repentance".

During Jesus' day, full-blown sinners came to repentance. The same thing happened during Wesley's day. Isn't it time for it to happen again in our day? If it is going to happen, Christians will first need to look at people as Jesus and John Wesley did — as candidates for the grace of God.

See also: Eph. 2:8-9, 1 Tim. 1:15, Titus 3:4-6

March 13
Read John 5:1-17

"See, you are well! Sin no more, that nothing worse may happen to you." v. 14

Jesus often linked sickness with sin. In His first encounter with the man at the Pool of Bethesda, Jesus dealt with the man's sickness. In his second encounter, he dealt with the man's sin.

Although sickness is not always a direct result of sin, at times it can be. In 1 Corinthians 11:30 Paul goes so far as to say that some have died as a result of their sin.

But if sickness can be a result of sin, we also read that health can result from obedience! Proverbs 3:7-8 says, "Fear the Lord and turn away from evil. It will be healing to your flesh and refreshment to your bones". The Lord is not only a God of healing, but One who will sustain our health as we obey Him.

See also: Gen. 38:7, Js. 5:16, 3 Jn. 1:2

March 14
Read John 5:18-23

"Truly, truly, I say to you, the Son can do nothing of His own accord, but only what He sees the Father doing. For whatever the Father does, that the Son does likewise" v. 19

Jesus was The Christ; Very God of Very God; Divinity Incarnate. At the same time, He was a man just like you and me. When He was on this earth, He lived in total dependence on the working of the Holy Spirit in His life. Every morning He awoke, He needed the Holy Spirit anew. Every moment He was dependent on help from above. This is how we need to live as well.

An amazing truth to ponder is that the same Spirit that empowered the Lord Jesus empowers us. The Christian life is not our working, but His. That is the secret to victorious living and effective service. The hymn writer put it this way:

Jesus giveth us the victory; He who overcame on Calvary,
Overcomes again in you and me. Hallelujah, Jesus gives the victory!

See also: Rom. 8:11, Eph. 3:20, Phil. 2:12-13

March 15
Read John 5:19-24

"Truly, truly, I say to you, whoever hears My word and believes Him who sent Me has eternal life. He does not come into judgment, but has passed from death to life" v. 24 [March Memory Verse]

This is a verse that every Christian should know. First it tells how one is saved — By hearing and believing. Second, it gives three distinctions of believers:

1. A present reality — We have eternal life right now in this present world.
2. A future destiny — Jesus personally took our judgment on the cross. We will never face the judgment of God.
3. A past certainty — We have already crossed over from the realm of death into the realm of life.

PS. This is the March memory verse—in my estimation, one of the twelve most important verses in the gospels. I urge you to memorize it.

See also: Rom. 6:23, Col. 1:13, 1 Jn. 2:25

March 16
Read John 5:25-29

"An hour is coming when all who are in the tombs will hear his voice and come out, those who have done good to the resurrection of life, and those who have done evil to the resurrection of judgment." v. 28-29

Have you ever visited a cemetery and pondered its significance? Every stone represents a life that was lived and is now ended. Every grave contains a body which once walked upon this earth — a person who lived and laughed and loved just as you do now.

But if Jesus is right and the Bible is true, the grave is not the final end of mankind. At death, the soul of a believer immediately goes to be with the Lord (See 2 Cor. 5:8). The grave is only a temporary resting place of the body.

Imagine that cemetery you last visited. Right now, the bodies of those who have died trusting Christ are sitting on launch pads! The day is coming when those in their tombs will hear a trumpet from Heaven, a shout of a mighty angel and the voice of Jesus Himself calling them to newness of life.

The greatest event of all mankind is drawing near. And that event is going to take place simultaneously in every grave yard around the world! The same voice that spoke creation into existence will speak new life into the dead, and they will live! AMEN!

See also: Job 19:25-27, Dan. 12:2, Phil. 3:20-21, 1 Thess. 4:15-18, Tit. 2:13

March 17
Read John 5:30-40

"You refuse to come to me that you may have life." v. 40

In 1830, a Philadelphia court convicted George Wilson of mail robbery and murder. Shortly before his scheduled execution, President Andrew Jackson offered him a full pardon. He refused the pardon and requested to be hanged. The warden contacted the president. The president called for a Supreme Court decision. Chief Justice John Marshall declared a pardon is not a pardon unless it is received. George Wilson died on the gallows.

Just because Christ's atoning death made salvation available to everyone doesn't mean that everyone is saved. Have you personally received the pardon he offers?

See also: Acts 13:46, Heb. 2:3, 1 Jn. 2:2

March 18
Read John 5:39-47

"I have come in my Father's name, and you did not receive me. If another comes in his own name, you will receive him." v. 43

To turn away from Christ is to turn to an antichrist. To turn away from truth is to turn to a lie. To turn away from light is to turn to darkness. To turn away from life is to turn to death. Sadly, people every day do just that.

Some reject Christ by active rebellion. Others reject Him by passive neglect. But God in His mercy is still pursuing them. It is not too late for your loved one to come to Christ. God's grace is not exhausted by our sin. Long after we have given up on people, God is still pursuing them. Nevertheless, "today is the day of salvation". Come to Him today.

See also: Rom. 5:20, 2 Cor. 6:2, 2 Tim. 4:3-4, 2 Pet. 3:9

March 19
Read John 5:39-47

"If you believed Moses, you would believe Me; for he wrote of Me. But if you do not believe his writings, how will you believe My words?" v. 46-47

Sadly many people flounder in their faith because instead of believing what Moses wrote about creation, (Genesis 1-3) they have swallowed the lie of evolutionism. Therefore they have an impotent, chaotic (small "g") god who is incapable of helping them. They will never be vibrant in their faith until they realize that Genesis is absolutely true and scientific.

The night I met Christ as my personal Savior, I also met Him as my personal Creator. To try to separate the two would be a distortion of who He is. To discover that I was created by God's plan and purpose and design revolutionized my entire life — and it will do the same for you!

See also: Col. 1:15-17, Heb. 1:1-3, Rev. 4:11

March 20
Read Mark 2:23-28

"The Sabbath was made for man, not man for the Sabbath" v. 27

The giant Sequoia trees of California grow to be over 300 feet tall. With the tremendous pressure exerted on them when the wind blows, God provided a special way to keep them from blowing over.

Surprisingly, the roots of the Sequoia tree do not go very deep into the ground. Just below the surface, they fan out in all directions and intertwine with roots from other trees. Each tree literally needs other trees in order to stand. But together it is impossible for them to fall.

It is far from drudgery for the church to gather together. Through our intertwining with one another, each one helps the others to stand! That is at least one example of how the Sabbath was made for man! See ya Sunday!

See also: Ex. 20:8-11, Heb. 10:25

March 21
Read Matthew 12:15-21

"This was to fulfill what was spoken by the prophet Isaiah" v. 17

The word fulfill or fulfilled is used fifteen times in Matthew. He is constantly linking the events of Jesus' life to Old Testament prophecies.

Maybe you have seen lists of Old Testament prophecies that were fulfilled in the New Testament. But the words 'luck' and 'chance' are never found in the Bible. In fact, the Hebrew language had no word for luck. That concept was foreign to their thinking.

Everything that happens ultimately comes from the grand design of God. He is working in the details of our lives today to fulfill His plan for us personally. What a comfort to know that He is using even the hard times to fulfill His plan for us. Let us rest in that fact.

See also: Rom. 8:28, Phil. 2:12-13

March 22
Read Mark 3:13-19

"And He appointed twelve…that they might be with Him and that He might send them out to preach" v. 14

The order of events in Jesus calling His apostles is very significant. Before He gave them authority or sent them out to preach it was imperative "that they might be with Him". Someone has said that there is no witness without 'withness'.

Later, we see these same apostles boldly proclaiming the message of salvation and "they recognized that they had been with Jesus" (Acts 4:13). If we are going to make an impact on this needy world, our first priority must be that we spend time with Jesus. To be a leader of men you must first be a follower of Jesus.

See also: Acts 4:8-13

March 23
Read Luke 6:12-16

"And when day came, He called His disciples and chose from them twelve, whom He named apostles" v. 13

A bumper sticker reads, "Christians are not perfect, just forgiven". That is only partially true. To claim the title of Christian goes far beyond mere forgiveness. Webster's dictionary defines a Christian as one "having the qualities demonstrated and taught by Jesus Christ, such as love, kindness, etc." That is quite a standard to live up to!

A Christian is described as: a <u>mind</u> through which God thinks, a <u>heart</u> through which God loves, a <u>voice</u> through which God speaks, and <u>hands</u> through which God helps (Copied). To claim the name of Christian carries with it awesome responsibility! Let us who name the name of Christ live in a manner worthy of the title 'Christian'.

See also: Acts 11:26, Eph. 4:1, 2 Tim. 2:19, 2 Tim. 4:17

March 24
Read Matthew 5:1-10

"Blessed are the poor in spirit, for theirs is the kingdom of Heaven" v. 3

Man's value system and God's value system are very different — as different as God's vs. man's definitions of success. One of the greatest condemnations in the Bible was written to the Laodicean church in Revelation 3:17 — "You say, 'I am rich, and have prospered, and I need nothing, not realizing that you are wretched, pitiable, poor, blind, and naked." They trusted in their self-sufficiency and self-righteousness. But the poor in spirit are those who recognize their need before God.

Are you poor? Are you rich? That depends on if you ask God or man. Here is another paradox of the Bible — When you are poor in spirit, you are very rich! Indeed, a kingdom is yours!

See also: 2 Cor. 8:9, Js. 2:5, Rev. 2:9, Rev. 3:17

March 25
Read Matthew 5:1-10
"Blessed are those who mourn, for they shall be comforted" v. 4

Does it sadden you when you see a loved one turn his back on God? Are you grieved at the times when you have disappointed God? Does it break your heart to see things happen that break the heart of God? Then you are blessed!

There is a thing that I call "redemptive suffering." That is when our hearts are broken for a godly cause or when we endure hardships for His cause. Even if things don't turn out as we hope in this life, God has promised that in Heaven we will have His eternal comfort (Romans 8:18).

See also: Gen. 6:5-6, 2 Cor. 1:3-4, Js. 4:8-10, Rev. 21:4

March 26
Read Matthew 5:1-10
"Blessed are the meek, for they shall inherit the earth" v. 5

Meek: That doesn't sound like a term that we would want to describe ourselves. It is associated with timidity and cowardice. But if Jesus was meek (Mt. 11:29), and Moses was meek (Num. 12:3), what does meekness mean?

A good example of meekness is found in a rodeo horse used in calf roping. For the event, the cowboy wants a meek horse — one that is well trained; one that obeys his every command; one that is sensitive to the slightest pull of the reins.

To be meek means to be totally submitted to and courageously obey the One over you. It means that your will is fully surrendered to your superior. To those who are meek toward God, He has promised they would inherit the earth! Wow! Let's do it!

See also: Ps. 37:11, Phil. 2:7-8

March 27
Read Matthew 5:1-10

"Blessed are those who hunger and thirst for righteousness, for they shall be satisfied" v. 6

Are you a hedonist? Sadly, many people in America are. Hedonism is a philosophy that the chief goal in life is to be happy and indulge in pleasure. This is not a biblical concept. Indulgence in pleasure does not satisfy. Nor does it please God.

It is more important to God that we be holy rather than that we be happy. Jesus didn't die for us to make us happy, but to make us holy. Happiness (a more biblical word would be 'joy') is a byproduct of holiness. And the way to be holy is to hunger and thirst for righteousness.

And what is righteousness? It is not a state of perfection that only a limited few can attain. Whenever I see the word 'righteous' in the Bible, I substitute the phrase, "A right relationship with God". When you have that, you will be satisfied!

See also Ps.17:15, Ps. 23:3, Eccl. 12:13, Eph. 5:18

March 28
Read Matthew 5:1-10

"Blessed are the merciful, for they shall receive mercy" v. 7

Both naturally and spiritually God has put the laws of sowing and reaping into effect: 1. You reap _what_ you sow. 2. You reap _later_ than you sow. 3. You reap _more_ than you sow. Jesus tells us to sow mercy. When we do, we will reap the same.

God is not stingy in giving His mercy to us. The hindrance comes in our refusal to give it to others. When we have a disposition of mercy toward others, it places us in a position to receive mercy from God.

Mercy is a beautiful attribute of God. Give it to others, and His mercy will be displayed in your heart!

See also: Lam. 3:22-23, Gal. 6:7-8

March 29
Read Matthew 5:1-10

"Blessed are the pure in heart, for they shall see God" v. 8

Do you want to see God? Both in the future and right now, do you really want to see Him? Then you must be pure in heart.

Our nation today is obsessed with ecology, the environment, the food we eat and the water we drink. We wash our clothes, brush our teeth and shower all for the sake of cleanliness. But we are not nearly as concerned about moral pollution which we allow into our homes and hearts through television, the internet and numerous other devices. Contamination of the mind and soul is much more of a problem than environmental concerns. We cannot allow these pollutants in our hearts if we want to see God. If we want to see Him, moral purity is essential.

See also: Ps. 24:3-5, 1Tim. 5:2, Heb. 12:14, Js. 3:17

March 30
Read Matthew 5:1-10

"Blessed are the peacemakers, for they shall be called sons of God" v. 9

When people think of you, do they think of God at the same time? Do they say, "Now he/she is truly a Christian?" Do you identify with Christ to the degree that when they see you, they also see Him? When they see the peace of God in you, do they see the God of peace at the same time?

During Daniel's time, a heathen king named Darius said, "The God of Daniel...is the Living God" (Daniel 6:26). May people say the same thing of our God when they look at us! An old chorus from my college days goes as follows:

Let the beauty of Jesus be seen in me;

All His wonderful passion and purity;

O Thou Spirit Divine, all my nature refine,

'Till the beauty of Jesus be seen in me.

Let us then go forth displaying His beauty as we help others to find the peace of God and the God of peace.

See also: Jn. 1:12, Rom. 8:14

March 31
Read Matthew 5:13-16

"You are the salt of the earth, but if salt has lost its taste, how shall its saltiness be restored?" v. 13

    Are you a thermometer Christian or a thermostat Christian? Let me explain.

    A thermometer simply reflects the environment it is in. It has no influences on its surroundings, but rises or falls according to its environment. A thermostat, on the other hand, has an influence on its surroundings. It will not allow the temperature to drop beyond a certain point, but keeps its environment stable and warm.

    If you are a thermometer Christian, you may be pleasant and warm on Sunday morning, but cold and indifferent throughout the week. If you are a thermostat Christian, you are influencing the world around you with the spiritual warmth of the Savior.

    Are you a thermometer or a thermostat?

See also: Phil. 2:15, 1 Pet. 2:12

April 1
Read Matthew 5:14-16

"You are the light of the world. A city set on a hill cannot be hidden. Nor do people light a lamp and put it under a basket, but on a stand, and it gives light to all in the house" v. 14

    I remember in Vietnam complaining to God about being the only person in my squadron who was living for the Lord. It was very difficult from morning to night, day in and day out enduring vile language and fornication. I complained to God. His answer came in one simple question: "Why do you think I put you here?"

    If God has put you in a dark place, you are supposed to be a light! In John 8:12, Jesus said He was the light of the world. In Matthew 5:14, He said we are the light of the world. As Jesus was in the world, so we now are in the world. He came in a physical body. So we now are His body on earth.

    Jesus told us the two places we are to bear His light: First, <u>publicly</u>, as a city on a hill and second, <u>privately</u>, as a lamp in a house. Letting our light shine is essential for both areas.

See also: Is. 9:2, Acts 13:47, 1 Pet. 2:9, 1 Jn. 1:5-7

April 2
Read Matthew 5:17-20

"Do not think that I have come to abolish the Law or the Prophets; I have not come to abolish them but to fulfill them" v. 17

There are two eternal things in our midst — the human soul and the Word of God. My forever soul will exist some place for all eternity. When my soul comes in contact with the Word of God, and that Word is received, my soul is then destined for Heaven.

The ceremonial law was fulfilled in Christ and in His work on our behalf. Therefore, we never again need to make blood sacrifices or sin offerings. But the moral law is to be fulfilled day-by-day in our lives as we live for Him. Let us be good examples of the Word becoming flesh in us as we live among others today (John 1:14).

See also: Is. 40:8, Rom. 8:4

April 3
Read Matthew 5:17-20

"For I tell you, unless your righteousness exceeds that of the scribes and Pharisees, you will never enter the kingdom of heaven" v. 20

Let's take a trip to Hawaii. But instead of taking a boat or plane, let's swim! Let's go to San Francisco, jump in the ocean and start swimming.

If we did that, I know I wouldn't even get one-hundred yards. You may get a whole mile. Someone else may get even ten miles! But no one is able to swim all the way to Hawaii.

In a much greater sense, the same thing is true in attaining to the righteousness of God. You may do a few more righteous things than I do, but none of us can come to the full perfection required to be accepted by God. That is why we need a Savior.

The righteousness that God requires is not achieved; it is received. It is His righteousness given to us. It is not more of the righteousness of the Pharisees, but a brand new righteousness. You can have all the righteousness of Christ by simply asking.

See also: Gen. 15:6, Acts 10:34-35, Rom. 4:3, Phil. 3:9

April 4
Read Matthew 5:43-48

"But I say to you, love your enemies and pray for those who persecute you" v. 44

Paul urged Timothy that "supplications, prayers, intercessions, and thanksgivings be made for all people, for kings and for all who are in high positions..." (1 Timothy 2:1) When he made that exhortation, Nero was on the throne in Rome. No doubt those first century Christians did pray. But what happened to their prayers? Nero continued persecuting the church as sheep brought to the slaughter. It wasn't until the Edict of Milan in 313 under Constantine that Christians were accepted.

It is my belief that prayer is never wasted. I think prayers are stored up in Heaven just like water is stored up in the clouds to be poured out wherever God desires. Perhaps God did not immediately answer the prayers of those first century saints. But could it be that He stored them up to move the heart of a different king, even Constantine?

Prayer releases spiritual energy into our world. God always hears the cries of His children and responds. His delays are not His denials. Let us not cease to pray for our leaders no matter what they do.

See also: Eph. 6:19, Rev. 8:3-4

April 5
Read Matthew 6:1-4

"Beware of practicing your righteousness before other people in order to be seen by them" v. 1

When actor Carroll O'Connor who played Archie Bunker was interviewed, it was found that his views in real life were very different from those he portrayed on television. On television, he was a Republican. In real life, he was a Democrat. In front of the camera, he was politically conservative. In real life, he was liberal. He was only playing a part on television which was not him at all.

The term 'hypocrite' which is used in our text today literally means 'play actor'. It was the term used for Greek and Roman stage-actors. Their entire purpose was to be seen and heard by men.

The purpose of the Christian is to gain an audience with God, not with men. If our purpose is otherwise, we have our reward — man's acclaim — but no reward from our Father in Heaven.

See also: 2 Tim. 3:8, Jude 1:12

April 6
Read Matthew 6:5-8

"When you pray, you must not be like the hypocrites. For they love to stand and pray in the synagogues and at the street corners, that they may be seen by others" v. 5

A great orator was asked to deliver the prayer at a large fashionable church. His prayer was so eloquent! After the service, a member came to him and said, "That was the best prayer ever prayed to our church!" Question: If the prayer was prayed to the church and not to God, of what value was it?

I am not against written prayers. The Psalms are written prayers. But Charles H. Spurgeon said that God loves home-made prayers best. There is something about home-made cookies, or a home-made quilt, or a home-made card that is so much better than the store-bought ones. God feels the same way about our prayers. Even if it isn't quite perfect, offer your home-made prayer to God. That is the kind He loves best!

See also: Ps. 50:15, Eph. 6:18, Phil. 4:6-7

April 7
Read Matthew 6:5-8

"When you pray, go into your room and shut the door and pray to your Father who is in secret. And your Father who sees in secret will reward you" v. 6

A few years ago, my wife and I visited a hydroelectric plant on the Missouri River. We marveled at the mighty power produced when the water plunged over the generators, providing electricity for thousands of households.

If the water moving downstream produced such power, there must have been a force which raised that water to higher elevations in the first place. That power — evaporation. Just as there are hundreds of tons of water pouring over those generators every day, so there are also hundreds of tons of water being lifted by evaporation every day and being dropped as rain. Though the process may be unnoticed, nevertheless it still goes on.

Prayer is much like the process of evaporation. Though it may be unnoticed, it is still taking place from the hearts of God's people. When God moves in powerful ways, let us remember to thank Him for the ones who started the process by praying for us. Then let us continue the process by praying for others.

See also: Rom. 8:26-27, Rev. 5:8

April 8
Read Matthew 6:9-15

"Pray then like this..:" v. 9

We are told by our Lord how to pray. His pattern of prayer can be broken down as follows:

"Our Father in Heaven"	As a child to his father
"Hallowed be Your Name"	As a worshipper to his God
"Your kingdom come"	As a citizen to his king
"Your will be done…"	As a servant to his master
"Give us…our daily bread"	As a beggar to his benefactor
"Forgive us our debts"	As a sinner to his Savior
"Lead us not into temptation"	As a pilgrim to his guide
"But deliver us from evil"	As a captive to his deliverer (Copied)

See also: Ps. 5:2, Ps. 102:1, Js. 5:16-18

April 9
Read Matthew 6:16-18

"When you fast … your Father who sees in secret will reward you" v. 17-18

Fasting is a forgotten practice in the American church. It is defined as, "A temporary devotion of one's energies to prayer and spiritual communion." From the words of Jesus, it is clear that He expected His followers to practice fasting.

Some of the rewards of fasting are found in Isaiah 58:6 — "Is not this the fast I choose: to loose the bonds of wickedness, to undo straps of the yoke, to let the oppressed go free, and to break every yoke?" When we hear of people going on hunger strikes for various causes, it should challenge us to fast for God's purpose of breaking yokes of bondage in the lives of other people. Perhaps you know someone who is under the bondage of sin. If you have a burden on your heart for that person, the Lord may challenge you to fast as an expression of your concern. He has already promised to reward your sincere request.

See also: Is. 58:3-12, Acts 13:2, Acts 14:23

April 10
Read Matthew 6:19-21

"Do not lay up for yourselves treasures on earth" v. 19

An old miser who was about to die instructed his servant to take all his money and put it in the attic so when he died he could take it with him. After he died, they went upstairs and found all his money neatly stacked just the way it was left. His acquaintances determined that if he was going to take his money with him, they should have put it in the basement!

Man does not think or reason like God. One of the chief things we should do with money according to the Bible is to give it away. When we do, it is transformed from something of temporal value into something of eternal value. The money you give is still yours, but the account is changed from earth to heaven. How are your eternal investments?

See also: Josh. 7:10-26, Phil. 4:14-19

April 11
Read Matthew 6:22-24

"No one can serve two masters ... You cannot serve God and money" v. 24

I grew up just down the road from a little boy who was cross-eyed — really cross-eyed! Thankfully, doctors were able to correct his problem. But when playing together, I never could be certain whether he was looking at me or not. One eye would look at me, while the other eye would look at my brother beside me.

Many times we come to God as cross-eyed Christians with divided loyalties. We look at Him with one eye, but with the other eye we are looking at the things of the world. God may ask of us just as I asked of my little friend, "Are you looking at me or not?" Money is to be our servant, not our master. Let's keep both eyes focused on the Master.

See also: Ps. 119:113, Js. 1:5-8, Js. 4:8

April 12
Read Matthew 6:25-34

"Your heavenly Father knows that you need them all" v. 32

Old Testament Israelites had an excellent concept of the true God. But Jesus introduced a new concept —that of the fatherhood of God. We are part of the family with God Himself being our Father.

If you had a good father as you were growing up, you are blessed. Some had poor examples of what a father should be. Others had no example. Regardless of your past, through faith in Christ you now have a Father in Heaven who cares. He has promised that even if our parents abandon us He will receive us (Psalm 27:10). He knows your needs. And He promised to provide for you.

See also: Ps. 68:5, 2 Cor. 6:18, Js. 1:17, 1 Jn. 3:1

April 13
Read Matthew 6:25-34

"But seek first the Kingdom of God and His righteousness, and all these things will be added to you" v. 33 [April Memory Verse]

"All these things will be added…" Can this verse provide someone who has virtually no money with a car?

When I was first saved I began attending church in Anchorage, Alaska. It was quite an inconvenience for people to drive all the way out to the Air Base to pick me up. Just beginning to discover rich truths in the Bible, I came across Matthew 6:33. So I prayed and asked the Lord for a car. In His working through very specific circumstances, I was able to get my first car for $100. I sold it two years later for more than I paid for it.

This verse also got me through college debt free!

This verse is extremely practical. It was for me. And it can be for you too if you put God first in everything. Try it!

See also: 2 Cor. 9:10, Phil. 4:19

April 14
Read Matthew 7:1-5

"Judge not that you be not judged" v. 1

This verse certainly has been abused by those who don't want to be accountable to others. To take the place of God and condemn someone is a sin. But to discern an error and want to correct it is a gift. Indeed if all 'judgment' were wrong, we would never get the speck out of our brother's eye (v. 5). The difference between judgment and discernment is the attitude of the heart. Do you want to lovingly help others or do you want to condemn them? Truthfully answering that question will clarify which side of the good/evil divide you are on.

See also: 1 Cor. 6:2-3, Gal. 6:1

April 15
Read Matthew 7:1-6

"Do not give dogs what is holy, and do not throw your pearls before pigs, lest they trample them underfoot and turn to attack you" v. 6

At first glance, it appears that verse 6 is out of context with the passage. But here is the context: Don't judge (v. 1-5). But don't naively trust everyone either (v.6).

Often Jesus would tell His disciples or those He healed not to tell anyone what had happened (Matthew 8:4, 9:30, 12:16, 17:9, etc.). He knew that if certain people knew what He said or did, it would only be a hindrance to His ministry. The enemies of truth would use His words and deeds against Him. The same is true today. We shouldn't necessarily say everything we know to everyone who wants to hear. If the person is a dog or a pig (Jesus' words, not mine) don't trust him.

See also: Rom. 16:17-18, Phil. 3:18-19

April 16
Read Matthew 7:7-11

"Ask, and it will be given to you; seek, and you will find; knock, and it will be opened to you" v. 7

In the early 1800's four Indians (three from the Nez Perce tribe and one from the Flathead tribe) traveled some 2000 miles from their home in Montana to St. Louis. They made the trip because they heard that "The white people away toward the rising sun had been put in possession of the true mode of worshipping the Great Spirit (and) they had a Book that contains directions". No doubt we will see these four seekers of truth in Heaven!

Jesus said that everyone who seeks finds. If you do not yet have the peace of knowing that you have met the Lord, keep seeking. He has promised that He will be found by you.

Ps. The acrostic for this verse is: A — Ask
S — Seek
K — Knock

See also: Jer. 29:13-14, Jer. 50:4-5, Hos. 10:12

April 17
Read Matthew 7:7-11

"If you then, who are evil, know how to give good gifts to your children, how much more will your Father who is in Heaven give good things to those who ask Him!" v. 11

I asked for strength that I might achieve; I was made weak that I might obey. I asked for health that I might do greater things; I was given grace that I might do better things. I asked for riches that I might be happy; I was given poverty that I might be wise. I asked for power that I might have praise from men; I was made weak that I might feel my need of God. I asked for all things that I might enjoy life; I was given life that I might enjoy all things. I received nothing that I asked for, but all that I hoped for; My prayer was answered! (Copied)

See also: Rom. 8:26, 1 Tim. 2:1-2

April 18
Read Matthew 7:12-14

"Enter by the narrow gate. For the gate is wide and the way is easy that leads to destruction, and those who enter by it are many. For the gate is narrow and the way is hard that leads to life, and those who find it are few" v. 13-14

"Would you tell me, please, which way I ought to go from here?" That was Alice's question to the Cheshire Cat in Lewis Carroll's 'Alice in Wonderland'.

"That depends a good deal on where you want to go to," said the cat.

"I don't much care where," said Alice.

"Then it doesn't matter the way you go," said the cat.

The Bible makes it clear that if you want to get to God, it does make a difference which direction you take. There is only one way, and Jesus Himself is that way. Those who have put their trust in Christ have found that He truly is the way, the truth and the life (Jn. 14:6). Are you a follower of the Way?

See also: Deut. 6:4, 1 Tim. 2:5

April 19
Read Matthew 7:24-27

"Everyone who hears these words of mine and does them will be like a wise man who built his house on the rock" v. 24

Several huge mansions were built on the side of a mountain in California, overlooking the sea. Such a beautiful sight they were. And such a beautiful view they had. A few years later, excessive rains caused mudslides. Though the materials in the house cost hundreds of thousands of dollars, the foundations were not secure and the great mansions began sliding down the mountain. What a sight they were sitting there at an angle!

A greater tragedy is a life which may be built on the best education and training the world can offer, but is not based on the sure foundation of the Word of God. But thank God that no flood or rain or wind can destroy our house if it is based upon obedience to His Word.

See also: Ps. 1:1-6, 1 Cor. 3:11

April 20
Read Matthew 7:24-27

"Everyone who hears these words of mine and does not do them will be like a foolish man who built his house on the sand" v. 26

Psalm 14:1 and Psalm 53:1 both say the same thing — "The fool says in his heart, 'There is no God'". Notice that he says it in his heart, not in his head. A reasonable look at nature tells us that there is a God. Denying God is not a matter of the intellect but of the heart.

Who is a fool? It is not someone who lacks knowledge, but someone who rejects truth. The fool in Jesus' parable had enough knowledge and ability to build a house. But he didn't do it according to the truth that was staring him in the face. Ignoring truth has dire consequences.

A person doesn't need great intellect to be wise. He simply heeds and obeys the Word of God.

See also: Prov. 1:7, Prov. 12:15, Rom. 1:18-22

April 21
Read Luke 6:20-26

"Blessed are you who weep now, for you shall laugh" v. 21

After Herod had the children of Bethlehem killed, Matthew 2:18 tells of Rachel weeping for her children and refusing to be comforted. She had no doubt been the talk of Bethlehem, for she had young children (plural). But now they were all dead. Probably the scene of the soldiers breaking into her home and killing them before her eyes played over and over in her mind for the rest of her life. The biblical narrative then moves on, leaving poor Rachel to weep alone without comfort.

Whatever happened to Rachel? We are not told. But eventually she died. She closed her eyes in death and opened them in Glory to see her children again in the presence of their Redeemer. And for the last 2000 years she has been laughing! And no doubt Herod, as Luke 6:25 says, has been mourning and weeping.

See also: 2 Sam. 12:19-23, Ps. 30:5, Rev. 21:4

April 22
Read Luke 6:27-31

"But I say to you who hear, love your enemies, do good to those who hate you, bless those who curse you, pray for those who abuse you" v. 27-28

God and good are taken from the same root word. Devil and evil are taken from the same root word. Each has only one letter change between the two.

Someone has said, "I will not allow anyone in this world to reduce me to the point of hating him". How do we respond when others abuse us? Do we respond in kind with evil? Or do we get our cues from God and respond with good?

> To return evil for good — That's satanic
>
> To return evil for evil — That's human
>
> To return good for evil — That's Divine!

See also: Prov. 20:22, Is. 55:8-9, Rom. 12:17-21

April 23
Read Luke 6:32-38

"Be merciful, even as your Father is merciful" v. 36

Imagine if we were driving down a road and we came across a car in the ditch with a man trying to push it out by himself. We could say, "That poor guy. I hope he gets out. I feel so sorry for him." But if we drove on by without helping him we would have shown no mercy. Even praying for him wouldn't be an act of mercy. No action means no mercy.

Mercy is not a feeling, but an action. It is always expressed in practical ways.

Before His incarnation, Christ sat enthroned in the highest Heaven. But in His mercy, He did not just sit there and feel sorry for us pitiful creatures here on earth. Mercy moved Him to leave His throne, come to earth and give His life for us. Mercy acted!

God wants to show His mercy to others through you and me. Will you today take the mercy freely given to you and offer it to others in practical ways?

See also: Js. 2:14-17, 1 Jn. 3:17-18

April 24
Read Luke 6:43-45

"The good person out of the good treasure of his heart produces good, and the evil person out of his evil treasure produces evil" v. 45

I can go to that erotic website, laugh at that off-color joke, look at that seductive magazine, listen to that song with suggestive lyrics, and it doesn't affect me—or does it?

Psychologists tell us that everything we have heard, seen or done is still in our memory bank. Although we may not be able to instantly recall every thought we have ever had, those thoughts have entered into our subconscious and become part of our personalities.

Our lives are lived in our thoughts. Wrong actions always begin with wrong thoughts. Conversely, good actions are the result of good thoughts. That is why we need to have transformed minds through the working of God's Word and Spirit.

See also: Gen. 6:5, Rom. 12:1-2, 2 Cor. 10:5

April 25
Read Luke 6:46-49

Why do you call me 'Lord, Lord', and not do what I tell you? v. 46

A song depicting the way Jesus may respond to hollow praise without heartfelt commitment goes as follows:

> "You call me Lord and obey me not
> You call me the Bread of life and eat me not
> You call me the Way and walk me not
> You call me the Truth and believe me not
> You call me the Life and live me not
> You call me the Master and serve me not"
> (Then comes the most fearful line of all) —"If I condemn you, blame me not."

To become our Savior cost Jesus his life. But if He is going to be our Lord, it will cost us our lives! He took his cross for our sake. Now He calls us to take our cross for His sake.

See also: Josh. 24:15, Gal. 6:14, Phil. 2:8-11, Phil. 3:7-8

April 26
Read Matthew 8:5-13

"I too am a man under authority, with soldiers under me. And I say to one, 'Go', and he goes, and to another, 'Come,' and he comes, and to my servant, 'Do this,' and he does it" v. 9

This centurion was under the command of Caesar. His authority wasn't vested in himself, but in the one who was over him. As he submitted to Caesar, he had the authority of Caesar. Therefore any command he gave had the backing of Caesar himself.

The centurion looked at Jesus and realized that He too was a man under authority — the authority of God. Being submitted to God, He had the authority of God. Therefore any power that Jesus had was from God. And certainly God could take care of the problem this soldier had. All Jesus had to do was give the word, and his servant would be healed!

True followers of Christ have submitted themselves to the authority of Christ. Therefore, we also have Christ's authority! (Did you get that!?) Christ has all authority, and we are submitted to Him! Therefore, as we submit, we have His authority! I hope this truth keeps you awake tonight as you ponder it!

See also: Eph. 1:19, Eph. 3:20, Col. 1:11

April 27
Read Luke 7:11-17

"As He drew near to the gate of the town, behold, a man who had died was being carried out" v. 12

Two processions met at the gate of the city of Nain. One was a procession of joy. The other was a procession of sorrow. One was a procession of life. The other was a procession of death. The central figure in one procession was a dead man. The central figure in the other procession was The Lord Jesus.

As the two processions met, one would need to give way to the other. Natural thought tells us that the funeral procession should take precedence. Shouldn't the followers of Jesus step aside and reverently let the mourners continue? But Jesus reversed natural order. He spoke to a dead man! And the dead man lived! The procession of sorrow and death was transformed into a procession of joy and life! In Jesus, life prevails over death!

See also: 1 Cor. 15:53-57, 1 Thess. 4:15-18

April 28
Read Matthew 14:1-12

"He sent and had John beheaded in prison" v. 10

Adultery and murder are linked together in the Bible. They are also often the main vices portrayed in many of our modern-day movies. Where we see adultery, murder follows close behind. David, after his sin with Bathsheba, had her husband Uriah killed (2 Samuel 11:1-26). Herod had John the Baptist killed because of his 'wife' Herodias. Today people have abortions for the sake of their adulterous ways. In each case, innocent people suffer because of the activities of the wicked.

The end result of fulfilled lust is still discord and death. Only fools would be deceived to think otherwise. We need to know that love and lust are not synonyms but antonyms. God has given His commands out of love. He wants to protect us from the bitter consequences of lust. Let's follow God's way — the way of faithfulness and purity.

See also: Ex. 20:13-14, Rom. 13:9

April 29
Read Matthew 12:22-32

"Whoever is not with Me is against Me, and whoever does not gather with Me scatters" v. 30

We are in the midst of a spiritual war of cosmic proportions. The church and the world are on a collision course. They cannot peacefully coexist. Jesus was not crucified because He uttered the pleasant platitudes of a dreamer, but because His words condemned the world.

In America today, the philosophy of secularism and the Christian faith are vying for supremacy. One of the two mindsets will eventually dominate our culture. Jesus made it plain that we cannot be morally and culturally neutral. To fail to make a whole-hearted commitment to Christ is to cast our lot against Him. To drift along on the current of contemporary culture is to decide against Christ.

There is a battle going on for the souls of men. Which lifestyle will dominate your heart; that of the world or that of Christ?

See also: Eph. 6:12, Js. 4:4, 1 Jn. 2:15-17

April 30
Read Matthew 12:33-37

"I tell you, on the day of judgment people will give account of every careless word they speak, for by your words you will be justified, and by your words you will be condemned" v. 36-37

"Now that you have confessed your brother's sins, are there any sins of your own that you would like to confess?" That was the question presented to a professing Christian after slandering another believer.

The end result of evil words is not what they do to the person who is spoken against, but what they do to the soul speaking them. Your words are being recorded. You will answer for them. Our daily prayer should be that of the psalmist when he said, "Set a guard, O Lord, over my mouth; keep watch over the door of my lips" (Psalm 141:3)

See also: Rom. 3:13-14, Js. 3:2-12

May 1
Read Matthew 13:1-9

"And He told them many things in parables, saying: 'A sower went out to sow'" v. 3

In Jesus' parable of the sower, He divided mankind into four groups: The hard-hearted, who hear the word of God but do not receive it; The faint-hearted, who after receiving the word do not endure; The half-hearted, who allow other things to take precedence over the word in their lives; And the whole hearted, who obey God's Word and become productive in the Kingdom of God.

Only one of the soils was productive. The other three proved to be worthless. When God looks at your life and mine, which type of soil are we?

See also: Acts 17:11, Heb. 10:36

May 2
Read Mark 4:1-9

"As he sowed, some seed fell along the path, and the birds came and devoured it" v. 4

The parable of the sower has given me more insight than any other parable that Jesus spoke. The four different soils represent four different responses people have to God's word. The seed by the path (also v. 15), represents a self-centered person. His life revolves around himself. He is his own god. Because of this, the Word of God never penetrates into his heart. When he walks out of church, everything is forgotten before he gets out the door (Literally!). You can expect to encounter this type of person as you give out God's word. Don't feel that you have failed him. That is just the way some people are. Let God deal with him and go to the next person.

See also: 2 Thess. 3:2, Heb. 4:2

May 3
Read Mark 4:10-19

"When tribulation or persecution arises on account of the word, immediately they fall away" v. 17

The seed (Word of God) is sown on four different soils. The Path represents <u>self-centered</u> people. The rocky ground represents <u>people-centered</u> people. The thorny soil represents <u>money-centered</u> people. And the good ground represents <u>God-centered</u> people.

When Jesus spoke of rocky soil, He was referring to just a few inches of soil with a layer of rock under it. These people are more interested in what others say and think than in what God says and thinks. They are more influenced by other people than by God. They are controlled by emotions rather than reason. These poor weak-willed, weak-rooted people.

Ask God to make you strong so your life would be controlled by the Word of God rather than other people.

See also: Prov. 29:25, Gal. 6:9, Heb. 10:39

May 4
Read Mark 4:14-20

"The ones sown among thorns...are those who hear the word, but the cares of the world, and the deceitfulness of riches and the desires for other things enter in and choke the word" v. 18-19

My father decided that he was going to break up some land and make a field bigger. "That's good soil," he said. "How do you know?" I asked. "You never raised a crop on it". "It's good soil", he said. "Just look at the brush it grows!"

There are many very good people who are doing nothing but growing brush on their land! Oh, the things that they accumulate that are only going to rust and burn. There are times when God decides to break up or burn the thorny field so it can produce an eternal crop. Please be on guard against being a money-centered person.

See also: 1 Cor. 3:12-15, Heb. 6:7-9

May 5
Read Mark 4:14-20

"But those that were sown on the good soil are the ones who hear the word and accept it and bear fruit, thirtyfold and sixtyfold and a hundredfold" v. 20

How would you like to have a thirtyfold increase on your investment? Or sixty? Or a hundred?! It sounds better than the guy with the thorns who got everything burned! If you are going to have great increase /eternal increase, Mark 4:20 says you must do three things: 1. Hear the word, 2. Accept it and 3. Bear fruit. If God is the center of your life you will bear fruit for eternity. That is what we were appointed to do (John 15:16). As we are faithful, God will make us fruitful.

See also: Rom. 1:13, Gal. 5:22-23, Col. 3:23-24

May 6
Read Matthew 13:10-15

"You will indeed hear but never understand, and you will indeed see but never perceive" v. 14

"I'm going to take my boys to the doctor," said the father. "Why?" I asked. His answer —"Because they don't hear".

The exasperated father knew that the problem was not with his sons' ability to hear, but with their willingness to listen. They were like so many of us (or should I say all of us?) who get distracted by other voices around us and forget which voice we should listen to.

Jesus said many times, "He who has ears, let him hear". God has given us spiritual ears and is constantly trying to communicate with us. Perhaps there is something right now that you know God is saying to you, but thus far you have been unwilling to listen. Please be eager to listen today. And remember, listening includes obeying.

See also: Heb. 3:7-8, Heb. 3:15-16, Js. 1:19

May 7
Read Matthew 13:31-35

"The kingdom of Heaven is like a grain of mustard seed that a man took and sowed in his field" v. 31

When I was in Israel, I got some mustard seeds. They are about as big as a period at the end of a sentence. I put them under a piece of tape on a 3x5 card —just little black specks. If you dropped one in the dirt you would never find it again. Yet it grows to be a tree.

Of what significance is the church as compared to the national government? How important is the Gospel compared to Wall Street investments? How does having a Bible study impact the world compared to television news? About as much as a mustard seed.

The planting of the mustard seed was a deliberate act of the man in the parable. The message of Christ, though seemingly insignificant, will grow to be a tree that no one can ignore. Just wait and see. Meanwhile, let's keep planting mustard seeds!

See also: 1 Cor. 3:6-9

May 8
Read Mark 4:35-41

"And a great windstorm arose, and the waves were breaking into the boat... But He was in the stern, asleep" v. 37-38

The disciples were in the storm on the Sea of Galilee for one reason —because they chose to follow Jesus. They obeyed Jesus — they met problems. That dispels the idea that following Jesus means we will always have a calm and placid life. It also dismisses any thought that problems are always a result of disobedience.

Have you ever followed God and ended up in a squall? Worse yet, did He 'fall asleep' on you in the midst of your storm? You may feel God has abandoned you in your tough circumstances. But the ultimate purpose of God in allowing the wind and water to beat on your little boat is to strengthen your faith (See verse 41).

Where are you right now in your walk with Christ? ...entering the 'boat' of a new experience? ... facing a 'storm' alone? ...trying to 'wake up' Jesus? ...or experiencing the 'calm' after the storm? Wherever it is, remember that the center of His will is the safest place to be!

See also: Rom. 5:3-5, Rom. 8:28

May 9
Read Mark 5:1-20

"Go home to your friends and tell them how much the Lord has done for you, and how He has had mercy on you" v. 19

God wants to turn your mess into a message. He wants to turn your test into a testimony. Your personal testimony is how God took the worst things of your life and turned them into good. That story is uniquely yours. It is the story that will make people stop and listen and put their trust in the Lord.

After the man with demons was healed, he wanted to go with Jesus. But God had a better plan and sent him home. He went to the Decapolis (the ten cities) and told them what the Lord had done. As a result, 'everyone marveled' (v. 20). No doubt we will see the fruit of his testimony when we get to Glory!

See also: Acts 4:20, 2 Cor. 1:3-4

May 10
Read Luke 8:34-39

"Then all the people of the surrounding country... asked Him to depart from them... So He got into the boat and returned" v. 37

Jesus is a gentleman. He will not force His way into your life. He will not impose His will upon you. He has authority to expel demons. But He will never intrude on your free will. He has all power in the universe. But He has given you absolute freedom with the decisions you make. If you reject Him, He will leave without an argument.

Every place the gospel has gone some have accepted it and some have rejected it. To expel Christ from our lives means His presence, His blessings, His eternal life also leave. To accept Him demands submission to His will even if it goes against our nature. But He is a gentleman. He leaves the decision to us. The choice is ours.

See also: Is. 1:19-20, 2 Tim. 2:11-13

May 11
Read Matthew 9:27-31

"According to your faith be it done to you" v. 29

"I prayed and nothing happened. I didn't think it would." A person who would say such a thing is what I call an 'unbelieving believer'.

Throughout the Gospels, Jesus referred to people who had no faith, little faith, some faith, and great faith. True faith focuses not on our circumstances, nor on ourselves, but on our Savior. Perhaps the biggest mistake some people make is that they try to have faith in faith rather than faith in God. He is the object of our faith. The first question to ask is not 'How big is your faith?' but 'How big is your God?'

Jesus classified people as having no faith, little faith, some faith, and great faith. What would happen if He said to you, 'According to your faith be it done to you'?

See also: Heb. 11:1-2, Js. 1:6

May 12
Read Matthew 9:32-34

"But the Pharisees said, 'He casts out demons by the prince of demons'" v. 34

The only one who could give us victory over Satan was accused of having the power of Satan. Isn't it interesting how the enemies of Jesus always get things completely backwards? It is also interesting who protests when the evil one is defeated! These misguided religious leaders of Jesus' day revealed whose side they were really on.

May God grant us wisdom not only to know our authority over the forces of evil, but also to know how to respond to those who protest when evil is being rooted out.

See also: Eph. 6:10-17, Phil. 3:18

May 13
Read Luke 8:40-42, 49-56

"He said, 'Do not weep, for she is not dead but sleeping.' And they laughed at Him, knowing that she was dead" v. 52-53

If you are going to do a God-sized work for the Lord, someone is going to laugh at you. In fact, if someone isn't laughing, maybe your project isn't big enough. If you don't need the help of God to complete it, it certainly is too small.

The character trait most necessary for carrying out the will of God is courage. The ridicule of scoffers (especially church members and professing Christians) will try to rob you of your courage. Satan himself uses these people to try to stop the work of God. This is one of his chief tactics. It seems he can always find a scoffer to be his spokesman.

You must decide that you are going to listen to the voice of God, and not the voice of scoffers. Then resolutely go forward.

See also: Josh. 1:9, Neh. 4:1-5, 1 Cor. 16:13

May 14
Read Matthew 9:35-38

"The harvest is plentiful, the laborers are few; therefore pray earnestly to the Lord of the harvest to send out laborers into His harvest" v. 37-38

When Christians get together to pray, they often ask for prayer requests. With Jesus in the gathering, His prayer request would be that God would send out laborers into His harvest.

After getting a vision of the lostness of man and the great need on the mission field, a church elder began to pray that God would raise up laborers. His request began in general terms. Then in faith, he prayed, "Lord, send someone from this very church". After a moment of silence and spiritual struggle, he prayed, "Lord, send my daughter."

As a result of your prayer, God may raise up someone close to you to be used in a special way as one of His harvesters. He may even raise you up!

See also: Is. 6:8, Acts 9:15

May 15
Read Matthew 10:1-15

"He called to Him His twelve disciples and gave them authority…" v. 1

In Matthew 10:1 Jesus' followers are called 'disciples'. In verse two they are called 'apostles'. A <u>disciple</u> comes to Christ to learn. An <u>apostle</u> goes from Christ to teach.

In the narrow sense, an apostle is one who personally saw the risen Christ in the flesh. In a broader sense, each of us are to be apostles, giving out the message of Christ. We are called to be both disciples (learners) and apostles (teachers).

Who would God have you be an apostle to? Who is the one who will become a disciple because of your witness? In turn that person will be raised up to be an apostle to others! And the cycle goes on and on until we reach the entire world! Amen!

See also: Acts 1:8, Rom. 10:14-15, 2 Cor. 5:18-20

May 16
Read Matthew 10:5-15

"And proclaim as you go, saying, 'The kingdom of Heaven is at hand'" v. 7

In chronological terms, the kingdom of Heaven is near. Christ's return is closer now than it ever was before. It is also near in terms of distance. Christ is as close to every person on earth as He can be without violating their free will. He is not only in the highest heaven. Nor is He in some distant place. But He is just outside the door of our hearts. Christ stands, knocking and waiting at the heart's door of each person. To see others in that light will change our attitude toward them.

How about you? Have you made an active decision to open your heart's door to Him and invite Him in?

See also: Rom. 10:6-8, Rev. 3:20

May 17
Read Matthew 10:16-23

"Behold, I am sending you out as sheep in the midst of wolves, so be wise as serpents and innocent as doves" v. 16

Sheep, wolves, serpents, doves. This passage does not paint a very pretty picture of who we are in the world. We need to also be aware that both sheep and doves were used as sacrifices. In past centuries and in many lands today, people are martyred for the cause of Christ. Under those circumstances, we are told to arm ourselves with two things—wisdom and innocence.

Through it all, we are never promised a life of ease. We are serving in combat behind enemy lines. But always remember that we are promised victory, just as Christ was victorious.

See also: Rom. 8:31-39, Rom. 12:21, 1 Jn. 4:4, 1 Jn. 5:4, Rev. 12:11

May 18
Read Matthew 10:24-33

"Everyone who acknowledges me before men, I also will acknowledge before my Father who is in Heaven" v. 32

The Bible calls us to make two confessions. First we are to confess our sins to God. Second we are to confess our Savior to man. Both confessions are necessary for salvation.

There is something about confessing our Savior before men that gives us assurance of our own salvation. But even more than that, Jesus will personally speak your name before the throne of God! Your name spoken by the lips of Jesus will be heard by thousands upon thousands of angels. Ten thousand times ten thousand angels will know your name—perhaps they do already! The voice that spoke the universe into being will speak your name, and that voice will echo through all eternity forever and ever! AMEN!

See also: 1 Jn. 1:9, Rom. 10:9-10, Rev. 3:5

May 19
Read Matthew 11:25-30

"Take My yoke upon you and learn from Me ... for My yoke is easy, and my burden is light" v. 29-30 [May Memory Verse]

No two oxen have the same strength. The bigger, stronger one is hitched on the right, while the smaller, weaker one is on the left. Depending on the strength of each ox, the farmer hitches the load closer to the stronger one, so that he pulls the majority of the load.

As we are 'yoked' to Jesus, He obviously is the stronger of the two and hitched to our right. The load is hitched closest to Him, so He does the majority of the pulling. Essentially, all we need to do is walk beside Him and keep in step with Him. That makes our yoke easy and our burden light.

See also: Jer. 31:25, 1 Jn. 5:3

May 20
Read Matthew 13:53-58

"He did not do many mighty works there because of their unbelief" v. 58

God has infinite power. But His exercise of power in our midst is limited by our faith. We cannot resist the Spirit and be filled with the Spirit at the same time.

Contrast our verse today with Luke 5:17 —"The power of the Lord was with them to heal." What was the difference between the two situations? —The condition of the hearts of His audience. He is not going to force His way into our lives or impose His will upon us, even though His will is what is best for us. He will only do what we willingly allow Him to do.

See also: Acts 7:51, Eph. 5:18

May 21
Read John 6:1-14

"Andrew, Simon Peter's brother, said to Him, 'There is a boy here who has five barley loaves and two fish, but what are they for so many?'" v. 8-9

Lack of faith is a result of measuring human difficulty by human resources. But there was one in their midst, a boy, who was willing to surrender his small lunch (everything he had) to Jesus. And that was the time God could work!

The boy offered everything he had to Jesus. And Jesus took it all. Then He blessed it, and multiplied it 5000 times! Not only were the multitudes satisfied, but there were twelve full baskets left over — one for each of the disciples!

A lesson I learned long ago was that we should do what we can with what we have. Take what is in your hand and put it in Jesus' hand. It may be insignificant, or small in comparison to the need. But you won't see a miracle until you give it to Jesus.

See also: 2 Cor. 8:3-5, 2 Cor. 9:6-10

May 22
Read Matthew 14:13-21

"Then He broke the loaves and gave them to the disciples, and the disciples gave them to the crowds" v. 19

The feeding of the 5,000 is the only miracle mentioned in all four of the Gospels. I'll leave it up to you to figure out why.

When the Israelites were in the wilderness, God supplied them with manna. What a miracle — bread actually coming down from Heaven! Here, Jesus fed multitudes with only one basket of food. Another great miracle! But isn't it also a miracle that we can toss a few seeds in the ground and a few months later have more bread than we even need? Whether our bread comes down from Heaven or up from the ground or out of a basket, it is all a miracle from the hand of our great God.

The next time you have a slice of bread or a bowl of cereal, just think — God personally placed life into each seed that grew. He personally superintended the growth and development of each kernel. He knew which kernel you would eat while it was still growing in the field! Isn't that enough to make you pause before eating and give Him thanks?

See also: Gen. 1:29, Ex. 16:4-31

May 23
Read Mark 6:35-44

"And taking the five loaves and two fish, He looked up into Heaven and said a blessing and broke the loaves and gave them to the disciples to set before the people" v. 41

What is our responsibility as disciples of Jesus Christ? It is simply to take the bread from His hand and place it into the hands of others. His supply always comes with His call to us to meet the needs of others. All He expects of you is to do what you can with what He has given. As the disciples turned to Jesus for new supply, so we need to do the same. A very special blessing rests on us who are vehicles of His grace to others.

In what way does God want to use you as a channel of His compassion to others?

See also: 2 Cor. 9:10, Phil. 4:18-20

May 24
Read Mark 6:45-52

"Immediately He spoke to them and said, 'Take heart, it is I. Do not be afraid'" v. 50

The first emotion mentioned after the fall of man was fear (Gen. 3:10). Since then and to this very day, fear has played a powerful role in the heart of every person who ever lived. But every time there was an encounter by God or an angel with a human, the first words were 'Fear not'.

The acrostic for 'F-E-A-R' is: 'False – Evidence – Appearing – Real'. While some fear is legitimate, the wrong fear can paralyze our lives. Let's be sure that any fear we may have is according to truth and not according to false evidence appearing real.

See also: Ps. 23:4, Prov. 29:25, Is. 41:10, 2 Tim. 1:7, 1 Jn. 4:18

May 25
Read John 6:25-34

"Do not labor for the food that perishes, but for the food that endures to eternal life, which the Son of Man will give to you." v. 27

"It sure is funny," said the big construction worker, shaking his head. "My neighbor worked all his life digging stumps and clearing land. After he died, another guy bought it and planted it to trees".

How much of this life is really lasting? How much of what we do will really matter a hundred years from today?

Temporal activities are necessary to sustain ourselves in this world. But our major emphasis should be on the eternal. Although Jesus was a carpenter by trade, the only eternal thing he accomplished with wood and nails was to die for our sins. That is a far more valuable work than the feeding of the 5000—a miracle which met their needs for only one day.

What are you doing today that will really matter 100 years from today?

See also: 1 Cor. 3:11-15, 2 Pet. 3:10-13

May 26
Read John 6:35-40

"For this is the will of My Father, that everyone who looks on the Son and believes in Him should have eternal life, and I will raise him up on the last day" v. 40

A Christian man who had a brush with death from a heart attack was asked what his view of Heaven was like since that time. His answer was, "Heaven will simply be an extension of the eternal life which I already have".

In speaking of eternal life, Jesus always used the present tense. We have it because we have Him — right now! Eternal life doesn't begin when we die, but when we receive Christ. Eternal life is not a thing but a person. Our hope is as sure as the resurrection of Christ. And you can have this same assurance! All you need to do is: 1. Hear, and 2. Believe.

See also: 1 Jn. 2:25, 1 Jn. 5:20

May 27
Read John 6:41-51

"The bread I will give for the life of the world is my flesh" v. 51

When our grandson, Justin, was about three, he enjoyed "helping" me in the lawn. As he assisted me, the questions started coming:

"Whose picnic table it that?"

"It's mine."

"Why?"

"Because I made it."

"Whose lawn mower is that?"

"Mine."

"Why?"

"Because I bought it."

Why do we belong to God? First, because He made us. Second, because He bought us. Both answers are reason enough to give our entire being in service to Him.

See also: Ps. 139:14, 1 Pet. 1:18-19

May 28
Read John 6:66-71

"Simon Peter answered Him, 'Lord, to whom shall we go? You have the words of eternal life, and we have believed and have come to know, that You are the Holy One of God" v. 68-69

During the Korean and Vietnam wars, when soldiers got captured, many of them overcame overwhelming odds. But there were others who had no wound or injury, no sickness or disease, who just sat down in the corner of their cell and died — they literally died!

I have seen a similar phenomenon in a Christian context as well. A person who was walking with the Lord meets a little resistance and quits — just quits.

Many Christians need to be more far-sighted — to look beyond their immediate circumstances to the hope they have before them.

You may be weary of your pilgrimage. You may feel like a long distance runner who wants to quit. But remember, every runner who is running properly wants to quit — every one! But if you quit following Jesus, where will you go? Who else has the words of eternal life? Keep following Him.

See also: Acts 20:24, Heb. 10:39

May 29
Read Matthew 15:1-9

"He answered them, 'And why do you break the commandment of God for the sake of your tradition?'" v. 3

There are two forces which can be operative among the people of God — the Word of God and the tradition of men. Tradition is not always bad. We celebrate Christmas. We have certain traditions at Easter. Even Jesus celebrated the traditions of the Passover, etc. But when tradition takes precedence over the Word of God, it is wrong.

Even in 'Bible Churches' people can insist on a certain translation or a certain music style, which have a tendency to bring people into bondage instead of freedom. While certain externals may be highly valued in some churches, they may forget the greatest command of all — "You shall love the Lord your God with all your heart and with all your soul and with all your mind…and love your neighbor as yourself" (Mt. 22:37,39).

See also: 1 Sam. 16:7, Is. 55:8-9, Col. 2:8, 2 Thess. 2:15

May 30
Read Mark 7:1-8

"This people honors me with their lips, but their heart is far from me" v. 6

There is a vast difference between a hypocrite and a defeated Christian. 'Hypocrite' literally translated means 'play-actor'. It has the idea of a person on stage pretending to be someone he is not. His only purpose is to put on a show for an audience and gain their applause.

A defeated Christian, on the other hand, is not a pretender. Rather, he realizes that the outward acts of his life do not measure up to what he knows in his heart. There is great hope for such a person.

Jesus never called His disciples hypocrites. They may have been lacking in faith or going through struggles but they were not play-actors.

If you have given your heart to Christ, but are facing struggles, don't let Satan call you a hypocrite. You are not. Ask God for His strength in your situation. Soon you will be experiencing in your life what you know in your heart!

See also: 2 Cor. 12:9-10

May 31
Read Mark 7:1-8

"You leave the commandment of God and hold to the tradition of men" v. 8

In days long ago, a telephone operator would get a call every day just before noon asking for the exact time. Finally, one day the operator asked the man why he needed the exact time every day. The man explained that he blew the village whistle at noon and he needed the precise time.

The shocked operator exclaimed, "I set my clock by that whistle!"

We need to have a standard outside of ourselves to govern our lives. That is why God has given us His Word. Cultural norms and mores are in constantly changing. To govern our lives according to them will lead to problems we cannot imagine.

The Bible is always accurate. Read it. Let it govern your life.

See also: Ps. 119:110, 2 Cor. 10:12, 2 Tim. 3:15

June 1
Read Mark 7:9-13

"Thus making void the word of God by your tradition" v. 13

In our culture today, we seldom see many people abandoning God's Word for the sake of tradition. Today, people are forsaking God's word for the sake of contemporary thought and trends. The latest teaching, the latest idea, the latest fashion is what we chase after. We then fashion a 'god' that fits in with our whims; a 'god' that we can be comfortable with.

Psalm 119:89 says, "Forever, O Lord, Your word is fixed in Heaven". It is much better to hold to God's eternal word than to the passing fads of men.

See also: Is. 40:8, 2 Tim. 3:14-15, 2 Tim. 4:2-4

June 2
Read Mark 7:14-23

"For from within, out of the heart of man, come evil thoughts, sexual immorality, theft, murder, adultery, coveting, wickedness, deceit, sensuality, envy, slander, pride, foolishness" v. 21-22

Several years ago I took a fishing trip and came home without one fish. But I did have a few healthy minnows left over. So I took them out of their dirty, messy water and put them into my clean, pure aquarium. In the morning, my previously pure aquarium was as messy as the old minnow bucket the fish were in the day before. The problem was not in the minnows' environment, but in their nature. They had secreted a slime that ultimately brought them to a fate worse than the minnow bucket.

Today, we try to clean up society by stopping fights, cleaning up slums and ending crime. While these efforts are sincere, problems will continue until man's nature is changed. Our world will only change when we allow God to change us from within. Have you had that heart change?

See also: Ezek. 36:26, 2 Cor. 5:17

June 3
Read Matthew 16:5-12

"O you of little faith, why are you discussing among yourselves the fact that you have no bread?" v. 8

Jesus said that His disciples (the insiders) had little faith. In Matthew 15:28, the Canaanite woman (an outsider) had great faith. Isn't it amazing that someone outside the church can have more faith than someone inside the church! (Yes, it's true —I've seen it!)

The great leveler for mankind is not status or position—not even position in the church! The great question is whether or not we exercise faith. We error when we think that everyone inside the church door is fine and everyone outside is lacking. Perhaps some are not in the church because they have not seen faith in us!

See also: Prov. 3:5-6, Gal. 5:6, Heb. 11:6, Js. 5:14-16

June 4
Read Mark 8:22-26

"He looked up and said, 'I see men, but they look like trees walking'" v. 24

The only way anyone can become a Christian is by a supernatural touch from God. We can give people the light of God's word, but only a touch from Christ can give them sight. Often people come to Christ and find forgiveness for their sin. But they do not grasp the rich treasures of what He has for them. They need a second touch.

Perhaps Jesus has touched you once and you know that you are saved. But you do not have a clear vision of His will and His ways. Ask Him right now to touch you again.

See also: 1 Cor. 13:12 , Heb. 2:9

June 5
Read Mark 8:27-30
"And He asked them, 'Who do you say that I am?'" v. 29

Who is Jesus? To the architect, He is the Chief Corner Stone; To the baker, He is the Living Bread; To the banker, He is the Hidden Treasure; To the biologist, He is the Life; To the builder, He is the Sure Foundation; To the doctor, He is the Great Physician; To the educator, He is the Great Teacher; To the farmer, He is the Lord of the Harvest; To the geologist, He is the Rock of Ages; To the jurist, He is the Righteous Judge; To the jeweler, he is the Pearl of Great Price; To the lawyer, He is the Counselor; To the horticulturist, He is the True Vine; To the reporter, He is the Good News; To the philosopher, He is the Wisdom of God; To the sculptor, He is the Living Stone; To the servant, He is the Good Master; To the student, He is the Incarnate Truth; To the traveler, He is the True and Living Way; To the sinner, He is the Lamb of God who takes away the sin of the world! (Copied)

See also: Is. 9:6, Rev. 19:12, Rev. 19:16

June 6
Read Matthew 16:13-20
"On this rock I will build My church, and the gates of hell shall not prevail against it" v. 18

Jesus gave us three 'I will' statements which are as certain as life itself:

1. 'I will rise from the dead '—The 'I will' of the past (John 2:19)
2. 'I will come again' —The 'I will of the future (John 14:3)
3. 'I will build My church' — The 'I will' of the present (Mt. 16:18)

When these three 'I will's' are taken together we can see the full panorama of God's plan for planet earth. The certainty of Christ building His church is as sure as His resurrection from the dead. It is going to happen. It is happening today. When the church reaches its full stature, the 'I will' of His second coming will take place.
Only Christ could fulfill the 'I will' of rising from the dead. And only Christ can fulfill the 'I will' of returning to earth. But in fulfilling the 'I will' of building His church He has invited you and me to have a part. What a privilege!

See also: Rev. 14:14-16

June 7
Read Matthew 16:13-20

"On this rock I will build My church, and the gates of hell shall not prevail against it" v. 18

"I think that I can say without contradiction that when the Paris Exhibition closes, the electric light will close with it, and no more will be heard of it". So said Erastis Wilson, an Oxford professor in 1878.

Many people have predicted the end of the church. They say it will die of old age and irrelevance. But God has a different plan. His plan (and it will be fulfilled!) is to have a vibrant, witnessing church in every community, village and hamlet on earth.

If we want our lives to count for eternity, we need to find out what God is doing and get right in the middle of it. Though we are far from perfect now, Christ will perfect His church. His plan is to work mightily through it even to confront the gates of hell!

The electric light was not turned off in 1878. Neither will the light of the Gospel be extinguished! Let's get to work!

See also: Ps. 100:5, Eph. 4:11-15, Eph. 5:27, Rev. 19:7

June 8
Read Matthew 16:21-28

"Get behind Me, Satan! You are a hindrance to Me. For you are not setting your mind on the things of God, but the things of man" v. 23

Isn't it amazing that Satan (Yes, Satan!) spoke to Jesus through His most zealous disciple! And sadly at times today, he speaks through well meaning Christians.

God's agenda is totally different than man's. It is impossible to conduct God's work by carnal means.

God loves people who are zealous, like Peter. Lethargy never did anything for the cause of Christ. But zeal without knowledge is like a galloping horse without a bit. Let us be sure that our zeal is not misdirected. May God help us to have a perfect understanding of His will and ways when we speak or act.

See also: Job 1:6, Is. 55:8-9, Rom. 10:2

June 9
Read Matthew 16:24-27
"Then Jesus told His disciples, 'If anyone would come after Me, let him deny himself and take up his cross and follow Me'" v. 24

Everyone who walks through this life will deny something. We will either deny ourselves or we will deny Christ. If we deny Christ as Peter did, (Matthew 26:34) the end result will be bitter weeping and sorrow.

Sooner or later each of us comes to the point of decision between our will and the will of God. To choose our own way will lead to loss. But to choose the will of God will lead to life and peace. I urge you to deny yourself and choose God's will above your own.

See also: 2 Cor. 8:9

June 10
Read Matthew 16:24-27
"For what will it profit a man if he gains the whole world and forfeits his soul? Or what shall a man give in return for his soul?" v. 26

A party of hikers was stranded on a mountain during a snowstorm. They managed to find a shelter from the wind, but realized that if they didn't get a fire started they would freeze to death. They took matches from their supplies but what could they use for kindling? Finally they had an idea. Each of them reached into his pocket, took out his money and placed it on a pile. Then they lit the money on fire. Adding twigs and branches, they managed to stay warm until the storm broke.

Saving their money would have meant certain death. But sacrificing it on the fire preserved their lives. Have you realized the complete inadequacy of money and material things when it comes to your soul?

See also: 1 Tim. 6:7, 1 Pet. 1:18-19

June 11
Read Mark 8:33-38

"If anyone would come after Me, let him deny himself and take up his cross and follow Me" v. 34

The cross is at the same time both repulsive and attractive. In it we see both death and life, wrath and love, sin and righteousness, hell and heaven. It is the ultimate paradox.

It is not pleasant to admit our personal responsibility for Jesus' anguish on that cross. But if we are repelled by it, we will die. If we are attracted to it, we will find life.

To miss the cross is to miss everything. It is central in the Christian faith, central in history, central in Heaven, central in eternity and central in the plan of God. But is it central in your life? Have you owned it for yourself with both its shame and glory? Embrace it today and you will find life!

See also: 1 Cor. 1:18, 1 Cor. 2:2, Gal. 6:14

June 12
Read Mark 8:34-38

"What does it profit a man to gain the whole world and forfeit his soul?" v. 36

A businessman was told he could have any request he desired. He asked for the Wall Street Journal two weeks from today. His plan was to make a million dollars in the stock market. Upon reading the rest of the paper, he discovered his name in the obituary column.

The driving passion of some people is to spend money they don't have to buy things they don't need to impress people they don't like! Concerning our souls, Jesus made it clear that money is often more of a liability than an asset. We need to be ever vigilant against the love of money.

See also: 1 Tim. 6:10, 2 Tim. 3:2, Heb. 13:5

June 13
Read Luke 9:23-27

"If anyone would come after Me, let him deny himself and take up his cross daily and follow Me" v. 23

A saintly old lady was asked how she could live such a victorious life in spite of dire circumstances. Her surprising answer was, "Every day I have my own funeral." What this lady meant by her statement was that she was applying the truth of Luke 9:23 to her daily life. She daily considered herself to be dead to self and alive to God (Rom. 6:1-12). If we apply this truth to our lives, it will bring us the same results as it brought her. Our lives can be transformed into the reality of Jesus Himself living His victorious life in and through us! Please ponder this reality until it lives within you.

See also: Gal. 2:20, Eph. 2:4-7, Col. 3:1-4

June 14
Read Matthew 17:1-8

"(Peter) was still speaking when, behold, a bright cloud overshadowed them, and a voice from the cloud said, 'This is my beloved Son with whom I am well pleased; listen to Him'" v. 5

God is not our heavenly bellboy whom we ring up every time we want an errand run. He is not our buddy that we make deals with whenever we want a favor. He is Lord, Supreme over all the universe. He is King; we are subjects. He is Creator; we are part of His handiwork.

We have been given the privilege of prayer. But prayer is not an excuse to get God to do things our way. It is a reporting for duty; an appointment to receive Divine orders.

Yes, the Lord is an intimate friend. But at the same time, we must remember that He is Very God of Very God, the High and Holy One who inhabits eternity. There are times when we should do nothing in His presence except to bow in silence and awe. This is what the disciples had to learn when they stood on the Mount of Transfiguration. We also need to learn anew to "listen to Him".

See also: Ex. 3:5, Job 42:5-6, Hab. 2:20

June 15
Read Luke 9:28-36

"And a voice came out of the cloud, saying, 'This is My Son, My Chosen One; listen to Him'" v. 35

One of Jesus' favorite sayings was, "He who has ears, let him hear". What was Peter doing when the exhortation came from Heaven to listen? He was talking. What are we often doing when God is trying to speak to us? Talking. It is impossible to talk and listen at the same time.

Most certainly there is a time to talk — particularly when we speak for our Savior. But before we can say anything worthy of others' ears, we must heed the admonition to listen. All of us need to cultivate the practice of listening to God.

See also: Eccl. 3:1-8, Acts 28:28, Js. 1:19

June 16
Read Matthew 17:14-20

"Lord, have mercy on my son, for he is an epileptic and he suffers terribly" v. 15

The disciples had been on the mountain top with Jesus, and they had just seen Him radiantly transfigured before them. It was so extraordinary that Peter wanted to build tents and live there! This was the one event of Jesus' life that Peter referred to in his letter (2 Peter 1:16-18).

Mountain top experiences are so wonderful. But we don't live on the mountain of supernatural spiritual experiences. Jesus led His disciples back down into the valley. And there they met an epileptic: a boy that had problems, and a family who needed help.

Jesus came to earth to help people. And though we may at times have great spiritual experiences, most of our lives are lived in the valleys, where others need help. So let's not sit longing for great ecstasy. There will be plenty of that when we get to Glory. Let's go down in the valleys where people live and get to work helping others.

See also: Rom. 15:1-3, Js. 2:15-17

June 17
Read Mark 9:14-29

"Jesus said to him, 'If you can! All things are possible for one who believes'" v. 23

The Israelites exercised their faith by getting out of Egypt. But they did not have enough faith to get them to the Promised Land. Consequently, they wandered in the wilderness. Isn't that just like us? Maybe a good title for such people would be 'unbelieving believers'.

The issue at hand is not "what can God do?" but "what do I believe God can do?" We must be sure however that our belief is not presumption, but trust based on His character and His word.

Perhaps the day will come when a mountain will literally be moved by a word of faith as it says in Matthew 17:20. Until then our prayer should be, "I believe; help my unbelief." (v. 24)

See also: Eph. 3:20, Heb. 6:1, Heb. 11:1-2

June 18
Read Matthew 17:14-20

"Truly, I say to you, if you have faith like a grain of mustard seed, you will say to this mountain, 'Move from here to there,' and it will move" v. 20

To build the first suspension bridge across Niagara Falls was not an easy feat. The task began by flying a kite across attached to a light string. Then a slightly larger string was attached to the small string and pulled across. Next a small rope was attached to the string continuing the process. Next came a larger rope, and then a cable. By this means, the bridge was eventually built.

A mustard seed is smaller than the period at the end of a sentence. But like the light string, if acted upon, can grow to carry a bigger and bigger load. If your faith is only as big as a thread or mustard seed, act on it in spite of its size. As you do, it will grow, and eventually you will be able to move mountains and build bridges you never thought possible!

See also: Ps. 20:7, Is. 40:31, 2 Thess. 1:3

June 19
Read Matthew 17:24-27

"Go to the sea and cast a hook and take the first fish that comes up, and when you open its mouth you will find a shekel. Take that and give it to them for Me and for yourself" v. 27

Three institutions have been established by God: the family, government and the church. The institution of government was established in Genesis 9:5-6 just after the flood. I am sure that God does not approve of corrupt government. Nevertheless we are called to submit to it until our submission leads to disobedience to God. This includes paying taxes.

Why do we have this story of the coin in the mouth of a fish to pay taxes? Could it be that God is trying to tell us that when we have taxes imposed on us He will supply in a special way for us to pay? Perhaps He is illustrating to us that when we are faithful to Him, He will even supply our need to pay our taxes!

See also: Rom. 13:1-7, Phil. 4:19

June 20
Read Matthew 18:1-9

"Whoever causes one of these little ones who believe in Me to sin, it would be better for him to have a great millstone fastened around his neck and to be drowned in the depth of the sea" v. 6

During the Civil war, General Stonewall Jackson received a message from General Robert E. Lee, which read, "I wish to see you on a matter of not great importance". General Jackson saddled his horse and rode nine miles through a snow storm to meet his superior. He greeted General Lee with the words, "Anything you want is important."

Anything General Jesus says or wants should be of utmost importance to us. Especially if it is a message as dire as is given in our reading today. Read it again and let its words sink into your heart!

See also: 1 Cor. 6:9-10, Eph. 5:3-12, Col. 3:5-6, Rev. 21:8

June 21
Read Matthew 18:7-9

"Woe to the world for temptations to sin! For it is necessary that temptations come, but woe to the one by whom the temptation comes!" v. 7

Sexual temptations are epidemic in our world today. A radio program devoted to help men resist temptation is called "Every Man's Battle." Jesus said we need to take radical steps to resist this temptation (v. 9). Centuries earlier, Solomon warned his son about the same temptation. His words (Proverbs 5:1-23, 6:20-35, 7:1-27) are a 'must read' for all young men. Please read and heed these passages for your own safety. It is the one temptation that God tells us to run from.

I am sure God does not want us to literally cut off our hands (v. 8). But if we are unable to resist temptation, He may want us to cut off the cord to our television sets — literally!

1Timothy 5:2 helped me greatly when I was single. There are many Proverbs 7 women in the world. Jesus pronounced a 'woe' on such women. But a Proverbs 31 woman is a treasured find.

See also: Prov. 31:10-31, 1 Cor. 6:18-20, 1 Thess. 4:3-7, 2 Tim. 2:22

June 22
Read Matthew 18:10-14

"I tell you that in Heaven their angels always see the face of My Father who is in Heaven" v. 10

Abusing or offending a child is no small matter in the courts of Heaven. Even angels get involved! This verse is a strong indication that we have guardian angels. No doubt each of us can look back at certain events of our lives and feel that an angel has intervened on our behalf, protecting us in times of danger.

But the verse says that our angels are in Heaven, not down here with us. I want them down here, not up there!

If I understand the heavenly realms correctly, angels constantly stand before God, seeing His face, waiting for Him to give a command. And I believe that faster than lightning, they can be at our side with all the authority of God, to help and protect us. If you don't believe that, just pray the next time you have an emergency. Your prayer will be answered before you get it spoken!

See also: Is. 65:24, Dan. 6:22, Acts 27:23, Heb. 1:14, Heb. 13:2

June 23
Read Matthew 18:15-20

"If your brother sins against you, go and tell him his fault, between you and him alone. If he listens to you, you have gained your brother" v. 15

The primary law of the Kingdom of God is love. When the law of love is broken one of two other laws need to be applied: 1. The law of forgiveness, or 2. The law of confession. When someone has harmed me, I need to apply the law of forgiveness. When I have harmed someone else, I need to apply the law of confession. Either way, it is my responsibility to go to my brother and restore the relationship.

The purpose in going to a brother is neither to prove I was right, nor to say what he did was okay, but to restore the relationship. The relationship is truly restored when the bond between you is stronger than it was before the infraction.

Remember also that not every relationship will be restored. After Jesus rose from the dead, He did not go to His executioners and try to restore them. But the door should always be left open in the event that they would have a change of heart.

See also: Rom. 12:18, Gal. 6:1

June 24
Read Mark 9:30-37

"On the way they had argued with one another about who was the greatest" v. 34

Adam's chief problem was not that he was out of fellowship with his wife but out of fellowship with God (Genesis 3:12). Cain's major problem was not his contention against his brother, but against God (Genesis 4:8). The same was true with Jesus' disciples. And the same is true today. Discord with one another is merely a sign of being out of harmony with God. But when we truly get right with Him, the natural result is harmony with one another.

Just after Jesus predicted that He was going to the cross, His disciples got into an argument about who was greatest. But don't all of us at times try to force our own agenda on one another instead of walking in the will of God? What we all need to do is align ourselves with the Savior, not with one another. Trying to tune ourselves with one another without first harmonizing with God is an exercise in futility.

See also: Rom. 12:10, Phil. 2:3, 1 Pet. 3:8-12, 1 Jn. 4:20

June 25
Read Mark 9:42-50

"If your hand causes you to sin, cut it off. It is better for you to enter life crippled than with two hands to go to hell, to the unquenchable fire." v. 43

A wily little monkey lives in the tropics. Because of his shyness, he is almost impossible to capture. But the natives have discovered a way to capture him: They take a gourd, bore a hole in it and place some nuts inside. Then they lash it to a tree branch. When the monkey discovers the nuts in the gourd, he reaches in to get them. But with a clenched fist, he cannot pull his hand back out. With a greedy refusal to loosen his grip on the nuts, the little monkey becomes easy prey for the natives!

How many of us are just like the little monkey? We have our little fist clenched tightly around something we treasure. The way to find freedom and safety is to simply let go. But we are bound by our lustful appetite. Unless we loosen our grip and forsake the tasty morsel, destruction is inevitable.

If you are held captive by your lusts today, I urge you to forsake your tiny treasure and flee to God for refuge.

See also: 2 Tim. 2:22, Heb. 12:15-17, Jas. 1:14-15

June 26
Read Mark 9:42-50

"… Hell, where their worm does not die and the fire is not quenched" v. 48

Sheol is the Hebrew word for the place of the dead. Hades is its Greek equivalent. The word primarily used for hell by Jesus was Gehenna. It made reference to a valley south-west of Jerusalem where centuries earlier the Canaanites sacrificed their children to Molech. During Jesus' day, it was a garbage dump where dead animals and refuse from the city were thrown.

Is hell real or is it figurative language? Any time figurative language was used, it is because there were no natural words to describe the situation. Therefore, hell would be much worse than the words used.

'Worm never dies'; 'Fire never quenched'; 'Weeping and gnashing of teeth'; ' Outer darkness'; 'Eternal fire'. These are the words that Jesus used to describe hell. When people banish God from their lives, there is no other place to go than a place like this.

Psalm 2:12 says, "Kiss the Son, lest He be angry, and you perish in the way, for His wrath is quickly kindled. Blessed are all who take refuge in Him."

See also: Rev. 20:11-15

June 27
Read Matthew 18:21-35

"Then Peter came up and said to him, 'Lord, how often will my brother sin against me and I forgive him? As many as seven times?' Jesus said to him, 'I do not say to you seven times, but seventy times seven'" v. 21

God calls us to be administrators of mercy and grace. He and only He can properly administer vengeance (Romans 12:19). And the day will come when He makes all things right.

There are some sins against us that are so egregious that we live with their consequences every day of our lives. To forgive seventy times seven may mean that we need to forgive that same sin over and over. The perpetrator may have already left this world and been dead for several years. In that respect, forgiveness is not only an event but a process.

Has someone sinned against you and left wounds to your very soul? May God give you the grace to release that person to His justice.

See also: Gen. 18:25, Gen. 50:15-21, Rom. 12:19

June 28
Read Luke 9:51-56

"Lord, do You want us to tell fire to come down from Heaven and consume them?" v. 54

It is possible for Christ's followers to become God's spokesmen in reverse. Instead of bringing a message of forgiveness and grace, we bring condemnation and retribution. This can happen even while we speak the truth but not in love. It is possible to have a right attitude toward sin but a wrong attitude toward the sinner.

It is not right for us who have received forgiveness to turn around and judge others for whom Christ died. Jesus spoke strongly against this. A wrong attitude on our behalf repels people from the Savior rather than attracting them to Him.

Let us be careful that we pray for others rather than against them as the disciples did. Such a prayer will only receive Christ's rebuke.

See also: Acts 7:60, Js. 4:1-3

June 29
Read Matthew 8:18-22

"Foxes have holes, and the birds of the air have nests, but the Son of Man has nowhere to lay His head" v. 20

Jesus never slept on a bed as good as mine. He never had a pillow as nice as mine. He told us that the hole of a fox and the nest of a bird are more secure, more permanent than where he lived. His final days were spent camping out on the Mount of Olives. I wonder if He even had a sheepskin to pull over His shoulders at night. He probably used a stone for a pillow (literally!).

Sometimes we think it strange when we endure a few hardships. We question God and even think He has forsaken us. But why is it that we think things should be so much nicer for us than it was for our Savior?

Just as in ancient times, if God's kingdom is to be advanced today, it still means there will be enduring of hardships. It would be good for us to take heed to Paul's words to Timothy, when he said, "Share in suffering as a good soldier of Jesus Christ" (2 Timothy 2:3).

See also: Gen. 28:11, Acts 5:41, Phil. 3:8, 1 Pet. 2:21

June 30
Read Luke 9:57-62

"Lord, let me first go and bury my father" v. 59

The statement of this would-be servant was an oxymoron. If Jesus is Lord, then he can't say, "Me first". But a second look at the request makes Jesus seem harsh and insensitive. Was this request too much to ask?

In the Jewish culture, the man was not making a request concerning a dead father but a living one. Perhaps the father would continue to live for decades. The would-be disciple wanted to postpone Christ's call on his life until his father died.

Delayed obedience is disobedience. Passive obedience is not obedience at all. If we are given a command, we do not have the option of lightly disobeying.

See also: Rom. 12:11, Heb. 3:7-8

July 1
Read Luke 9:57-62

"No one who puts his hand to the plow and looks back is fit for the Kingdom of God" v. 62

In 1519, Hernando Cortez took eleven ships and 700 men and set sail for Vera Cruz in the name of Spain. After landing, he purposely set his ships on fire, dashing any temptation to return without accomplishing his mission. The men, seeing the ships burning in the harbor, knew there was only one thing they could do — go into the interior of Mexico and claim it for Spain. As a result, Mexico became Spanish territory and Spain became a world power.

What would happen if Christians would burn any easy retreat from advancing the cause of Christ? If you have put your hand to the plow and looked back, it is not too late. You can again take up the cause of Christ and do exploits in His name.

See also: Phil. 3:7-9, 2 Tim. 4:7-8, Heb. 12:1-2, Js. 1:4

July 2
Read John 7:37-44

"Whoever believes in Me, as the Scripture has said, 'Out of his heart will flow rivers of living water'" v. 38

Water was a very precious commodity in the ancient land of Israel. Often people would walk miles to get their daily sustenance. But when they found a faithful well, an entire community would be built around it. Everyone in the city knew the path to the well. In fact, it became a center of community social life.

Jesus said that if you believe in Him with all your heart, you would become like that well. People around you who thirst for God will come to you to have their thirst satisfied.

Get ready! God is about to bring someone across your path whom you can help.

See also: Is. 55:1, Is. 58:11, 1 Pet. 3:15

July 3
Read John 8:1-11

"Let him who is without sin among you be the first to throw a stone at her." v. 7

People today don't generally throw stones at one another. Figuratively, however, some people sure throw a lot of mud! And when they pick up mud to throw, they inevitably get some on themselves as well. In addition, their handful of mud may have a few 'stones' which leaves their victims bruised as well as dirty.

The worst weapon we can wield against someone is an uncontrolled tongue. I am certain that some people who have never shot a gun will stand before God guilty of shooting words with their mouths. Others who have never seen a switchblade will be guilty of cutting and stabbing words.

Each of us should often pray the prayer of the psalmist in Psalm 141:3—"Set a guard, O Lord, over my mouth; keep watch over the door of my lips".

See also: Ps. 140:3, Js. 3:2-12

July 4
Read John 8:1-11

"Neither do I condemn you; go, and from now on sin no more" v. 11

Finish this sentence: "If you sin, God is going to _____."

God is righteous and just. He cannot allow sin to come into His holy presence. But it comes as a surprise to some people that His desire is not to condemn us but to forgive us. If God had only one message for mankind, I believe it would be, "I forgive you." That is why He came to earth in the first place.

What should we tell children when they sin? We certainly should not say that it doesn't matter to God. But neither should we distort their view of Him by telling them that He is going to send them to hell. Christ came to forgive us, not condemn us. He loves us. He responds to our rebelliousness not in anger but in sadness.

How should we finish the above sentence? Perhaps this way: "If you sin, God is going to be sad."

When we hear in our hearts Christ's pronouncement of forgiveness, we will also hear him say, "From now on sin no more."

See also: Gen. 6:5-6, Eph. 4:30, Titus 2:11-12, 1 Pet. 2:24

July 5
Read John 8:12-20

"I know where I came from and where I am going" v. 14

Where did I come from? Where am I going? Why am I here? How should I live? Please take a few minutes to ponder those four questions. Your answers determine your world view. If your answers come from the Bible, then you have a "Biblical World View". If your answer doesn't come from the Bible, you have a distortion of reality no matter how often you go to church.

Many people sadly do not know where they came from or where they are going. That is a classic description of what the Bible calls 'lost'. Where did I come from? I was created in the image of God. He has a purpose for my life. Where am I going? I am destined for celestial glory with God. Why am I here? To glorify, please and enjoy my God. How should I live? It will take a lifetime to dig those principles out of Scripture and apply them to everyday living.

I came from God and am going to God. The first thing to do is align ourselves directly between those two points. Next is to walk daily in that alignment. That is what the Bible calls walking in the Light.

See also: Gen. 1:27, 1 Cor. 10:31, Phil. 3:20-21, Titus 2:12, 1 Jn. 1:5-7

July 6
Read John 8:21-30

"Unless you believe that I am He you will die in your sins" v. 24

There are three kinds of death: Spiritual death, Physical death and Eternal death (See Feb. 22).

Jesus said three types of people will experience eternal death: 1. The person who does not believe that Jesus is the Christ (John 8:24); 2. The person who will not repent (Luke 13:3); 3. The person who has not been born again (John 3:3).

When talking with your neighbor about Christ, remember these three points: 1. Does he in the depths of his heart acknowledge that the Creator God who existed from all eternity has come to earth in the form of the man, Jesus? 2. Has he indeed renounced his old way of life? 3. Has the Spirit of God entered his heart and so changed him to the point that he can say a new life has begun? Anyone answering affirmatively to these three questions will not experience eternal death, but in fact has eternal life. Amen!

See also: Gen. 2:16-17, 1 Cor. 15:26, 1 Cor. 15:54, Rev. 20:11-14

July 7
Read John 8:21-30

"He who sent Me is with Me. He has not left Me alone, for I always do the things that are pleasing to Him" v. 29

People usually make decisions based on one of four things: Culture (Everyone else is doing it); Tradition (That is the way it's always been done); Emotion (It just feels good) ; and Reason (This seems the most logical).

The best way to govern our lives, however, is to determine what would be pleasing to God. When we seek to obey His Word out of a heart of love He has promised that His special presence would be with us. The closer you get to God through obedience, the closer He gets to you.

See also: Eph. 4:1, Col. 1:10, Js. 4:8

July 8
Read John 8:31-38

"If you abide in My word, you are truly my disciples, and you will know the truth, and the truth will set you free" v. 31-32

There was a young mother who went into a state of depression for several weeks. Finally a friend gave her a booklet which explained to her the love of her Savior. Upon reading the booklet, a new joy radiated from her to everyone she met. A few months later, she slipped back into her old way of thinking and her depression returned.

Seeing his mother depressed again, and remembering the joy she once had, her little son ran to her bedroom, grabbed the booklet on God's love, and came running to his mother exclaiming, "Mommy, Mommy, it still says the same thing!"

There are times when our feelings simply cannot be trusted. That is when we need to walk by faith in the tried and true Word of God, knowing that it will set us free from emotional bondage.

See also: 2 Cor. 5:7, Gal. 5:1

July 9
Read John 8:31:38

"Jesus answered them, 'Truly, truly, I say to you, everyone who commits sin is a slave to sin" v. 34

According to the dictionary to sin is 'to break a moral law or principle through a willful act'. I define sin as anything I do independently of God. When we sin, Jesus said that ultimately we ourselves are the biggest losers. Sin always diminishes us and makes us less than God intended us to be. But thanks to the grace of God, sin does not have the final word.

To say I must sin is to deny my Savior

To say I cannot sin is to deceive myself

To say I need not sin is to declare my faith in Divine power

See also: Rom. 6:14, 1 Jn. 1:9, 1 Jn. 2:1

July 10
Read John 8:34-38

"If the Son sets you free, you will be free indeed" v. 36

In 1902, Orville and Wilbur Wright were the first to succeed in manned flight at Kitty Hawk, North Carolina. Did you ever see pictures of people attempting to fly before that time? They would tie huge wings to their arms and jump off cliffs to certain disaster. The force of gravity was simply too powerful to overcome.

Trying to overcome sin in our own power is much like man's early attempts to fly. To try to overcome the power of sin in our own strength is an exercise of futility. We are utterly helpless to have victory in our natural strength.

Many Christians simply give up trying to have victory over sin and say that they have to sin. But God intended that we have freedom from sin. By His power in us we need not live our lives as slaves to sin. But first we need to get desperate enough to call on Him in total dependence.

See also: Rom. 6:14, Rom. 8:2

July 11
Read John 8:39-47

"If God were your Father, you would love Me" v. 42

"You are of your father the devil" v. 44

How do we know if someone has the true God? By their attitude toward Jesus. And what if they don't love Jesus? Then they are of their father, the devil! I didn't say that—Jesus did. No wonder they crucified Him!

Jesus leaves no middle ground. His words are very clear. The true God is the Father of our Lord Jesus Christ. Every other god is a false god. Any contrary teaching is a false teaching. Either you love Jesus or you don't.

See also: 1 Jn. 4:14-15, 1 Jn. 5:12, 1 Jn. 5:20

July 12
Read John 8:48-59

"Jesus said to them, 'Truly, truly I say to you, before Abraham was, I AM'" v. 58

Jesus was claiming to be the great 'I AM' who met Moses at the burning bush (Exodus 3:14). He made seven "I AM" claims in the book of John that are exclusive only to Him:

'I am the bread of life…'	Jn. 6:51
'I am the light of the world…'	Jn. 8:12
'I am the door…'	Jn. 10:9
'I am the good shepherd…'	Jn. 10:14-15
'I am the resurrection and the life…'	Jn. 11:25-26
'I am the way, the truth and the life…'	Jn. 14:6
'I am the vine…'	Jn. 15:5

These are claims that Jesus and Jesus only could make. Anyone else making them would face sure ridicule. Each exclusive claim has an exclusive promise that goes with it. It would make a great Bible study if ever you are asked to teach. That right there is worth the cost of this book!
PS. Jesus never said He is living water or the water of life. He said He gives living water (Jn. 4:10-14).

See also: Rev. 1:8, Rev. 1:17-18

July 13
Read John 9:1-7

"We must work the works of Him who sent Me while it is day; night is coming when no one can work" v. 4

Someone has rightly said, "We will have all eternity to celebrate our victories. But we have only one hour before sunset to win them". Everyone has the same amount of time —24 hours per day. When someone says he doesn't have time to serve God, he is really saying that other things are more important than serving God.

We need to be taking advantage of every opportunity God gives us. He has given us each day for a reason. Let us be investing our days for eternity.

See also: Ps. 90:12, Eph. 5:15-17, 1 Thess. 5:5-8

July 14
Read John 9:1-9

"The neighbors and those who had seen him before as a beggar were saying, 'Is this not the man who used to sit and beg?' Some said, 'It is he.' Others said, 'No, but he is like him.'" v. 8-9

Did you hear about the old farmer who got saved? Even his cows know the difference!

There have been times when I have seen God change a person so much that everything about him is different. The change is from the inside out. "Transformation" is not too strong a word for the change that takes place. It is so remarkable that even his neighbors see the difference — and talk about it! It is an even greater joy when his wife and children respond in the same way to the Lord!

God specializes in changing lives. I know. He changed mine!

See also: 2 Cor. 5:17, Eph. 4:22-24

July 15
Read John 10:1-6

"The sheep follow Him, for they know His voice. A stranger they will not follow, but they will flee from him, for they do not know the voice of strangers" v. 4-5

Who is one of Christ's sheep and who is not? Those who are listening to His voice and following Him are His sheep. Those who refuse to listen or follow do not belong to Him.

A Turkish shepherd found himself surrounded by enemy soldiers who confiscated his sheep and started away with them. After they traveled across a valley and started up the next hill, the shepherd started to sing. Upon hearing his voice, the sheep bolted from their captors and ran back to their master!

In our world today, there are plenty of strangers seeking to confiscate God's sheep for their own selfish purposes. There is a big difference between shepherds and sheep-shearers! And believe me, there are plenty of sheep-shearers out there. But thank the Lord that in spite of the many voices in this world there is One that is different! Be certain that you are listening to His voice, and not another.

See also: Ps. 23:1-6, 1 Pet. 2:25

July 16
Read John 10:7-10

"The thief comes only to steal and kill and destroy. I came that they may have life and have it abundantly" v. 10

I once had occasion to see a talented artist at work. He would set up his easel and challenge someone from the audience to come up and make scrawling marks in the center of the canvas. After studying the marks a few seconds, the artist would take his pencil and draw a beautiful picture, making those scribbles the very center of his creation!

Jesus came to give us abundant life. He has the unique ability to take the scribble marks imprinted on the fabric of our lives and turn them into something beautiful! What a creative Creator we have!

Has someone carelessly scribbled on the canvas of your life? Take heart! The Master Artist of the universe is about to take up his pencil and produce from those careless lines a design of rarest beauty! Believe it!

See also: Gen. 50:20, Rom. 8:18, Rom. 8:28

July 17
Read John 10:11-18

"I am the good shepherd. The good shepherd lays down his life for the sheep" v. 11

The <u>Good Shepherd</u> died for us (John 10:11). The <u>Great Shepherd</u> rose from the dead on our behalf (Hebrews 13:20-21). The <u>Chief Shepherd</u> will return for us (1 Peter 5:4).

Psalm 22 depicts Jesus as the Good Shepherd. In Psalm 23 He is the Great Shepherd. Psalm 24 presents Him as the Chief Shepherd. (Now ain't that interesting!)

I am prone to get lost, to lose my way, to even forget where I am. If there is one picture of Jesus that I appreciate, it is the fact that He is my Shepherd. I am so glad to have Him as my Good, Great, and Chief Shepherd. Please read the passages mentioned and see if you agree.

See also: Ps. 48:14, 1 Cor. 15:3-4, Phil. 1:6

July 18
Read John 10:22-30

"My sheep hear My voice, and I know them, and they follow Me. I give them eternal life, and they will never perish, and no one can snatch them out of My hand" v. 27-28 [July Memory Verse]

The best way to hear the voice of God is to listen with your <u>eyes</u>! God seldom speaks to us in absence of His written Word. His primary way of communicating to us is through His written Word. The Spirit of God and the Word of God always work in harmony with one another. As we read, the Holy Spirit gives us understanding . Therefore, read your Bible. As you do, you will hear Him by listening with your eyes!

PS. This memory verse has six clauses. Memorizing it gets it into your head. Meditating on it will get it into your heart.

See also: Ps. 119:1-8, Heb. 4:12

July 19
Read Luke 10:1-20

"The seventy-two returned with joy, saying, 'Lord, even the demons are subject to us in Your name'" v. 17

Have you ever seen an incident in the Scriptures where Jesus was afraid of demons? Then why are His followers so fearful? Who is stronger, Jesus or demons?

It has been my experience that a demon is more like a pesky little fly buzzing around our heads than any full-blown possession. It is also my belief that all of us have had a demon bug us at times. Their only power is what we allow them to have. Take authority over them as the first disciples did —in Jesus' name.

In my experience, I have observed that most demons come around when people are living in sin or rebellion against God. Thus we can see a spirit of lust, a spirit of greed, a spirit of drunkenness, or a host of other addictions that we think are 'normal'.

There are two ways of dealing with demons — starve them out or cast them out. It is absolutely essential that a person repent of all known sin before dealing with an oppressive spirit. But as His followers we have God's authority in dealing with them. Let's use it!

See also: Acts 16:16-18, Jude 1:6

July 20
Read Luke 10:25-37

"But a Samaritan, as he journeyed, came to where he was, and when he saw him, he had compassion" v. 33

Samaritans came into existence after Assyria captured the Northern kingdom of Israel. They were Israelites who intermarried with foreigners. They were despised by the Jews because of their mixed blood line and their mixed up faith.

Jesus used the illustration of a Samaritan to show that even someone despised may have a more compassionate heart than a priest or a Levite. Truly the line of good and evil is not drawn between races or ideologies, but within every heart. Here is an example of a good heart of a Samaritan. "You go, and do likewise" (v. 37).

See also: 2 Kings 6:22, Rom. 12:20-21

July 21
Read Luke 10:38-42

"But the Lord answered her, 'Martha, Martha, you are anxious and troubled about many things, but one thing is necessary'" v. 41-42

Put yourself in Martha's shoes. How would you feel if a good friend of yours stopped in just before supper? That would be fine with most people. But what if He brought twelve of His buddies with him and they were all hungry? Martha had a big job on her hands!

You can often tell what a person's gift is by what bothers him. Martha was bothered because she had the gift of service, and she wanted do her very best in serving her Lord. Imagine the privilege of preparing a meal for Jesus Himself!

It is important that the work gets done. But there is something more important than serving Jesus, and that is to sit at His feet and learn from Him. This is the "one thing" that we should concern ourselves with rather than the "many things" that distract us from it.

See also: Ps. 27:4, Phil. 4:6-7

July 22
Read Luke 11:1-4

"Lord, teach us to pray" v. 1

Of what significance is prayer in the midst of our highly technological age? Of what significance was it in Jesus' day? Would He not have been better off arming His followers with swords and spears and shields? What was the place of prayer in the midst of Caesar's edicts and marching soldiers?

It has been said, "Prayer is power. He who is a stranger to prayer is a stranger to power". Ultimately, spiritual power always trumps natural power. That is shown by the fact that the Christian faith eventually triumphed over the Roman Empire.

Of what significance is a little band of believers who meets to pray? Much! Prayer releases the power of God into our environment. When we don't just say our prayers but truly pray, the Holy Spirit of God is operative in our midst. "Lord, teach us to pray. Amen"

See also: Phil. 4:6-7, Js. 5:16-18

July 23
Read Luke 11:1-13

"When you pray, say: 'Father, hallowed be Your name'" v. 2

The Bible tells of many different postures of prayer — hands raised, head bowed, standing, kneeling, prostrate, etc.

I was saved while I was in the Air Force. Interestingly, the military taught me a valuable lesson about prayer. The church where I was attending had a practice of standing when praying. When the pastor said, 'Let us pray', my GI heels would automatically snap together. My arms would drop stiffly to my sides, and I stood at full attention. It was as if I were meeting my commanding officer. In that posture, my heart attitude was not to make requests, but to report for orders. It was as if my whole being was waiting for a word from my Superior.

I am not advocating that we all stand at attention when we pray. But maybe our prayers would be more effective if we come before the High and Holy One to listen, not talk; to obey, not make requests; and to please Him rather than please ourselves.

See also: Is. 65:24, Eph. 6:18, 1 Jn. 5:14-15

July 24
Read Luke 11:24-26

"The unclean spirit …says, 'I will return to the house from which I came'" v. 24

It is not enough to simply be freed from a bad habit or attitude which we may have. The evil needs to be replaced with good. If we do not replace evil with good, a spiritual vacuum exists, which will eventually be filled again with evil. To be fixated on evil and determine to keep it out means that evil is still in control. The negative must be replaced by something positive. Righteousness needs to replace evil.

If you are trying to overcome a bad habit, ask yourself what good habit can take its place. Ask the Holy Spirit to work in the area of your life where the unclean spirit formerly worked. This is the way to spiritual health and permanent victory.

See also: Rom. 12:21, Gal. 1:23, 1 Tim. 1:13-14

July 25
Read Luke 11:27-32

"But He said, 'Blessed rather are those who hear the Word of God and keep it'" v. 28

I remember getting a model car for Christmas. I opened the box and went to work. The shiny little wheels excited me. So I dug through the box, found an axle and put a wheel on each end. But I soon discovered that with a wheel on each end of the axle, I couldn't put the axle through the frame. I discovered in a practical way the wisdom of the old saying, "When all else fails, follow instructions".

All of us have at times tried to take short-cuts rather than doing things God's way. As a result, we end up spending much time and energy later trying to fix what we have messed up. In putting together our lives it is always best to follow God's Instruction Manual, the Bible.

See also: 1 Sam. 15:22, Prov. 14:12, 2 Thess. 1:8, 1 Pet. 4:17

July 26
Read Luke 12:8-12

"And I tell you, everyone who acknowledges Me before men, the Son of Man also will acknowledge before the angels of God" v. 8

Two confessions are necessary to truly be right with God —Confess <u>your</u> <u>sins</u> to God and <u>your</u> <u>Savior</u> to man.

It is not easy to acknowledge Christ before a scoffing world. It is much easier at times to remain silent. But if you will acknowledge Him, the day will come when King Jesus will sit on His glorious throne and personally speak your name. And every angel in the universe will hear it! All the mighty hosts of Heaven will know who you are! The Divine speaking of your name will forever put you into the 'Who's-Who?' in heavenly realms.

You may not be well known here on earth, but your name will be forever known in Heaven. And it will all be because you have stated before men who Jesus is. Confess His name on earth and He will confess your name in Heaven!

See also: Rom. 10:9-10, Rev. 7:9-10

July 27
Read Luke 12:13-21

"Take care, and be on your guard against all covetousness, for a one's life does not consist in the abundance of his possessions" v. 15

If only I had another thousand dollars my problems would be solved. Though some would make a statement like that, it is not true. Often, the more money a family has, the more likely they are to get into financial problems. Also, more money does not translate into greater happiness. Another hundred dollars to a greedy person does no more good than another drink to an alcoholic.

If your outgo exceeds your income, then your upkeep will be your downfall. Financial freedom is simply living on less than you make. It is very liberating to experience.

If money was a problem for people in Jesus' day, imagine how much more of a problem it is to us! Particularly in our world today, we need to be applying Jesus' words to our finances. And may God grant you the liberty to be able to live in financial freedom no matter how much or little money you make.

See also: Eccl. 5:10, Eph. 5:5, Phil. 4:11-12, 1 Tim. 6:9

July 28
Read Luke 12:13-21

"But God said to him, 'Fool! This night is your soul is required of you, and the things you have prepared, whose will they be?'" v. 20

Have you ever stopped to think that your casket might already be in town? ...that the flowers for your funeral might already be blooming? What a terrible mistake for a person to try to fortify his eternal soul with temporal treasures!

Isaiah said to King Hezekiah, "Set your house in order, for you shall die; you shall not recover" (2 Kings 20:1). That day is coming for each of us. We have no assurance of tomorrow. Today is the only day we have. A temporal value system will only be a liability in the presence of a Holy God.

See also: Amos 4:12, 1Tim. 6:17, Js. 1:11, Js. 5:1-3

July 29
Read Luke 12:22-34

"Sell your possessions, and give to the needy. Provide yourselves with moneybags that do not grow old, with a treasure in the heavens that does not fail, where no thief approaches and no moth destroys" v. 33

"When will you be moving into the new building?" I asked the lady working at Wal-Mart. "In about a month" she replied. Then she added, "I have worked here since the store first opened. If I knew what to do back then, I would have invested all I had in Wal-Mart."

Some people just have a knack in knowing how to invest. Others of us are not so wise and never reap the benefits of good investments.

What are we investing in today that will really matter 100 years from now? How can we use our time and resources that they may count for eternity? What are we going to wish we had done differently when we leave this world? These are the questions we need to answer now, so that on that final day we may receive an eternal reward.

If we want the investments of this life to last forever, let us heed the words of Jesus today.

See also: 2 Cor. 9:6-10

July 30
Read Luke12:22-34

"For where your treasure is, there will your heart be also" v. 34

> Angels in their realms on high, Look down on man with wondering eye, That where they are but passing guests, They build such strong and sturdy nests,
>
> And where they hope to live for 'ay, They scarce take time one stone to lay. (Copied)

Jesus didn't put much value in stuff. The basic principle concerning material things is that God owns everything. One hundred percent is His and we are just stewards. How much of your money belongs to God? Answer: all of it!

The Bible often refers to the tithe (which means tenth) which should be set aside specifically for the Lord's work. Those who have applied the principle of tithing can attest to the fact that 90% under God's blessing will go farther than 100% without it. But please remember that the remaining 90% still belongs to God, and you are just a steward of it.

Do your giving while you're living; then you're knowing where it's going!

See also: Hag. 2:8, Mal. 3:10, 1 Cor. 4:2, 1 Tim. 6:7

July 31
Read Luke 13:1-5
"No, I tell you, but unless you repent, you will all likewise perish" v. 3

In the spring of 1980 Mt. St. Helens was beginning to rumble. The authorities once more made their way to Harry Truman's (not the president) mountain cabin to warn him of impending danger. Smiling, waving and closing his cabin door, once more he turned them away.

The next morning, molten rock covered the area where Harry Truman's cabin stood. It didn't make any difference that he thought he was safe in his cabin. The facts prove otherwise.

Jesus came to save us from impending death. The end of those who refuse to believe Him are just as real as that of Harry Truman. But those who heed His words find refuge in Him. Trust Him today!

See also: Rev. 20:15, Rev.21:8

August 1
Read John 10:31-39
"You, being a man, make yourself God" v. 33

People who refuse to believe end up seeing things just the opposite of what they really are. The Jews accused Jesus of being a man who made Himself to be God. If they were right, Jesus indeed was guilty of blasphemy as they said. But in reality, He was not man making Himself God. He was God who made Himself man!

What a sinful thing it would be for a man to exalt himself as God. (This is what the antichrist will do). But what a wonderful miracle that God, the creator and sustainer and ruler of the universe has become a man! The saying is true—"The Son of God became the Son of man so the sons of man might become sons of God!"

See also: Phil. 2:5-11, 2 Thess. 2:4, 1 Jn. 5:20

August 2
Read John 10:40-42

"John did no sign, but everything that John said about this man was true" v. 41

The Bible makes it clear that at the end of the age there will be many sign-seekers. And Satan will not disappoint them in their quest. Many think that signs and wonders is the standard by which to judge someone's spiritual standing. But Jesus called the sign-seekers 'evil and adulterous' (Matthew 12:39). But He said of John the Baptist, who performed no sign, 'there is none greater' (Luke 7:28).

Truth is more important than signs. And it ought to be recognized as such in the church. If not, find a different church.

See also: Deut. 13:1-3, 2 Thess. 2:9-10

August 3
Read Luke 13:31-35

"O Jerusalem, Jerusalem…How often would I have gathered your children together as a hen gathers her brood under her wings, and you would not" v. 34

Revival begins when we quit confessing other people's sins and begin confessing our own. It is wonderful to see when God moves in a service, and people who are broken before God confess their sins. But was Jesus ever broken over sin? Did He ever cry out in remorse over sin? The answer may surprise you— 'Yes!' However, it was not His own sins, but for the sins of others that grieved Him.

If I could repent for other people's sins, I would. But not even Jesus can do that. Each person must repent of his own sin. Nevertheless, we need to have the heart of Jesus when we see others turn their backs on God. We should never mention someone else's sin without having a tear in our eye.

See also: Rom. 9:1-3, Rom. 10:1

August 4
Read Luke 14:25-33

"Whoever does not bear his own cross and come after Me cannot be My disciple" v. 27

The Bible talks of two crosses: Jesus' cross and my cross.

A missionary told of a religious festival in Mexico during which the entire community turned out to celebrate. Everyone was to carry a religious symbol or token as they marched through the city. An enterprising young man seeking to make some money pulled his cart into the square and put up his sign — "Cheap Crosses."

In reality, a cross is not cheap, but very costly. To bear a cross means to suffer affliction and ultimately death to self as a result of following Christ. Anyone who will take up his cross must lay down his life for its sake.

Christ's challenge to anyone who would follow Him is 1. Count the cost, and 2. Carry the cross. But ultimately, eternal benefits outweigh any cost. Are you willing? If so, a crown awaits you! But in the dictionary, as in life, the cross comes before the crown.

See also: Gal. 6:14, Phil. 2:5-11

August 5
Read Luke 14:25-33

"Which of you, desiring to build a tower, does not first sit down and count the cost? v. 28

How much will it cost to be Christ's disciple? Everything! Be we rich or poor, well known or obscure, Jesus said that being His disciple would cost us everything — even our very lives.

Is this too much to ask? Not when we realize that every pursuit has a cost. The cost of serving a false god has the same price tag as that of following the true God. The man who pursues riches will leave it all behind. He who sets his heart on strong drink will eventually be consumed by alcohol. The pleasure-seeker eventually finds life empty and pointless.

We will not get through this life without cost. There is a cost for serving Christ. But there is a greater cost for not serving Him. Pay now or pay later. The choice is ours.

See also: 1 Kings 18:21, Phil. 3:10

August 6
Read Luke 14:25-35

"Therefore, any one of you who does not renounce all that he has cannot be My disciple" v. 33

Advertisers tell us that if you have a product to sell, the first thing the prospective buyer needs to do is realize his need for the product. Second, he needs to know the advantages of buying that product. Third, he must know the cost and be willing to pay it.

In the 'selling' of Jesus, there certainly is a need. People all around us need the grace of our great Savior and the salvation He provides.

There are also many advantages of becoming a disciple of Christ. We have the promise of sins forgiven, of eternal life, of personal guidance, of peace and joy, and much more. But if our needs are going to be met in Christ, and we are going to receive the benefits of owning Him, there is also a cost. Are you willing to pay the price He is asking in order to own His name?

See also: Heb. 11:8, Heb. 11:24-26, Rev. 7:13-14

August 7
Read Luke 15:1-7

"And the Pharisees and scribes grumbled, saying, 'This man receives sinners and eats with them'" v. 2

The title 'sinner' in Jewish culture meant that the person was a Jew but he wasn't practicing his faith. When others went to the synagogue on the Sabbath, he would go out and plow his field. When others went to the festivals in Jerusalem, he would take the day off and relax. He was still a Jew but he was not cultivating a relationship with his God. He was a 'sinner' more because of omission than of commission. If that is the definition of a sinner, then there certainly are many of them around us today.

It has been said that Jesus died for all the wrong people. How true! His mission was to save the last, the least, the lost. The amazing thing is not that I received Christ, but that He received me. The only qualification to come to Jesus is to admit you are a sinner. Both by commission and omission, I have sinned. That is why I need the Savior. How about you?

See also: Acts 10:34-35, Rom. 5:8, 1 Tim. 1:15

August 8
Read Luke 15:11-24

"He was longing to be fed with the pods that the pigs ate, and no one gave him anything" v. 16

The prodigal son began with much, and lost it all. He invested his resources in the pursuit of worldly pleasure, but instead of finding fulfillment, he was brought to the doorstep of starvation. Sin always leads us to such a state. It always leads us to want — never to the fulfillment it promises. The young man discovered the high cost of sin.

If your life has been ravished by sin, you need to do what the prodigal son did — genuinely repent and return to the Father. If you will, He is willing to receive you back right now.

See also: Is. 55:7, Ezek. 18:31, Rom. 6:23

August 9
Read Luke 16:10-13

"One who is faithful in a very little is also faithful in much, and one who is dishonest in a very little is also dishonest in much" v. 10

A young accountant was seeking employment at a bank. The bank president invited him to a cafeteria for an interview during the lunch hour. Going through the lunch line, the president noticed that the young man hid a pat of butter under his bread so he would not need to pay for it. Although the accountant's qualifications were very high, he was not hired because of this single act of dishonesty.

God is a good economist. He is not going to invest His spiritual treasures in unfaithful people. He is looking for our faithfulness in material things to see if we can be trusted with spiritual things. Is your character such that He can trust you to be faithful in your service to Him?

See also: 2 Chron. 16:9, 1 Cor. 4:1-2, Rev. 2:10

August 10
Read Luke 16:14-18

"But it is easier for heaven and earth to pass away than for one dot of the Law to become void" v. 17

In 1999 a list of the one hundred most influential people of the last Millennium was published. And who came out number one? Who had the most profound effect on the human race in the last thousand years? Answer: Johann Gutenberg, the inventor of the printing press! And the first book to be published in 1455 was the Bible! And, yes, it changed the course of history!

In speaking of his invention, Gutenberg said, "Yes, it is a press, certainly, but a press from which shall flow, in inexhaustible streams, the most abundant and most marvelous wine that has ever flowed to relieve the thirst of man! Through it, God will spread His Word. A spring of pure truth will flow from it; like a new star, it shall scatter the darkness of ignorance and cause a light hereunto unknown to shine amongst men." And that is exactly what happened during the Reformation.

Oh, the beauty of the 'spring of pure truth' we hold in our hands! But it does us no good unless we drink from it. Are you daily coming to the stream of God's Word to refresh your soul?

PS. Isaac Newton came in second; Martin Luther was third. All three men were Christians.

See also: Ps. 19:7-11, 2 Tim. 3:16-17, 2 Pet. 1:20-21

August 11
Read Luke 16:19-31

"In Hades, being in torment, he lifted up his eyes" v. 23

Jesus spoke more about hell than He did about Heaven. No doubt that is because of the awesome horror of such a place. Wish as we may, we cannot wish away the reality of its existence.

Reading the account of the rich man and Lazarus, we see that proper names are used. We can conclude, then, that this is a true story about real people in a real place. Perhaps Jesus' listeners even knew Lazarus and the rich man of whom He was speaking.

We also see that after his death, the man in Hades could still feel, think, reason, and communicate. His request for a single drop of water to be placed on his tongue could not be granted. Although Jesus told this story nearly 2000 years ago, the rich man is still in the place of anguish and torment today. How terrible! Whether he wants it or not, he has an eternal soul that will exist forever in this place of suffering.

Jesus considered this place of torment to be so bad that He got off His throne in Heaven, came to this earth and placed His cross between mankind and hell. People in hell will need to go around the cross to get there.

How about you? Are you trusting the Savior?

See also: Rev. 20:11-15

August 12
Read Luke 16:19-31
"He called out, 'Father Abraham, have mercy on me'" v. 24

How important is prayer to you? We never read that the rich man ever prayed when he lived on earth. But as soon as he left this world it is the only activity of any importance. He prayed to the right person. He prayed for the right thing. But he didn't pray at the right time. During his life, he considered himself to be self-sufficient and in need of nothing from God. What a tragedy to step out of time into eternity before realizing his need.

Let us treasure our ability to communicate to God through prayer. And let us come before Him with the greatest request of all — the request for mercy. But that request needs to be made on this side of the grave.

See also: Ps. 51:1, Micah 7:18

August 13
Read Luke 17:5-10
"The apostles said to the Lord, 'Increase our faith'" v. 5

F   Forsaking

A   All

I   I

T   Take

H   Him

When the apostles asked Jesus to increase their faith, His response was in effect, 'Increase your faithfulness'. Faithfulness is the only true test of faith. The mustard seed of faith must be translated into living, growing acts of faithfulness. Those who exercise true faithfulness, at the end of the day will say, "We are only unworthy servants, we have only done what was our duty" (v. 10).

See also: Rom. 10:17, Heb. 11:1-40

August 14
Read John 11:1-15

"When he heard that Lazarus was ill, he stayed two days longer in the place where he was" v. 6

When Lazarus became sick, his sisters did the logical thing; they sent for Jesus. But he delayed coming, which resulted in Lazarus' death. Later both of his sisters said, "Lord, if you had been here…"

Someone has said that God's delays are not his denials. We know that Jesus had the ability to come and restore Lazarus to health. But the delay brought death, which ultimately brought about an even greater miracle—the raising of Lazarus from the dead!

Have you been going through a struggle and it seems that God has forgotten you? Have you prayed, but no answer has come? If you have called out to God and He hasn't answered, it isn't because He is indifferent. He has an infinite love for you. His delay is because He wants to work a far greater miracle in your life than you are requesting — possibly something you will not fully realize until we are with Him in eternity. Trust Him even if in the present hour He is delaying.

See also: Prov. 3:5-6, Eph. 3:20, 1 Pet. 4:19

August 15
Read John 11:17-27

"I am the resurrection and the life. Whoever believes in Me, though he die, yet shall he live, and everyone who lives and believes in Me shall never die" v. 25-26

The resurrection is not an event; it is a person! Proper relationship with Him provides us with resurrection. We are not waiting for Christ to return to have resurrection life. Neither are we waiting to die to attain it. In Him, we already have it! Death for the believer is merely an extension of the resurrection life we already have. In Christ we are already crucified, buried, and raised never to die again! By faith, we can live in this world on the resurrection side of the grave! This is a secret that most Christians do not understand. It is the key—the only key—to victory over the power of sin in your life. Please keep searching until you find this truth.

See also: Rom. 6:1-12, Gal. 2:20, Eph. 2:4-7

August 16
Read John 11:38-44
"He cried out with a loud voice, 'Lazarus, come out'" v. 43

If you have repented of your sins and placed your faith in Jesus Christ, I say to you on the authority of God's written Word, the day is coming when you (whether in the grave or still alive) will personally hear the shout of the Son of God, and come forth to life eternal! The same voice that spoke the universe into being will speak your personal name, and you will be transformed in a moment of time!

If you are saved, you already have a redeemed soul. But on that day, your body will be redeemed as well. That is the Gospel. It is the blessed hope of the Christian. Death to the Christian is not gloom and despair. It is our graduation day into newness of life! Believe it!

See also: Job 19:25-27, 1 Thess. 4:15-18

August 17
Read John 11:38-44
"Take away the stone …Unbind him, and let him go" v. 39 & 44

Someone has said, "Christ alone can save the world, but Christ can't save the world alone". If His work is going to be done on earth, it needs to be done through His body, the church. The church is more necessary than most people think.

Only Jesus can call people to new life. There is no other voice in the world that can speak to a dead man and make him live.

Jesus gave His disciples one command before He raised Lazarus, and another one afterward. His first command — "Take away the stone". Before a person can be called to new life, the barriers need to be removed. This is the work of evangelism. His second command — "Unbind him…". This is the process of making disciples. These two things are what we do, not God.

Though removing grave stones and grave cloths may be as unsettling to us as they sound, we are called to these tasks so that people may find new life and new freedom in Christ.

See also: Acts 4:12

August 18
Read Luke 17:11-19

"Then one of them, when he saw that he was healed, turned back, praising God with a loud voice: and he fell on his face at Jesus' feet, giving Him thanks" v. 15-16

The founders of our country felt that giving thanks to God was so important that they made Thanksgiving a national holiday. But if the ratio is the same today as it was with the ten lepers, 90% of the people don't have a heart of gratitude. Romans chapter one tells us that the first step in falling away from God is having an unthankful heart (v. 21).

The priests of Old Testament times were instructed to make thank offerings to God. When they did, the smoke was like incense rising up to God. Many of the Psalms accomplish this purpose.

Please make it a habit of your life to offer thanks to God throughout each day. If you do, you will become a different person. Also, God will be happier hanging out with you!

See also: Ps. 50:23, Heb. 13:15

August 19
Read Luke 17:20-25

"The kingdom of God is not coming with signs to be observed ... The kingdom of God is in the midst of you" v. 20-21

Where is the Kingdom of God? Answer: Any place the will of God is being done. The future kingdom will be the political and physical rule of Christ on earth. But the present kingdom is the spiritual rule in the heart of any person who will allow Him in. If He rules supreme over your heart and will, then indeed "The kingdom of God is within you" (v. 21). There is no external sign of this. We cannot tell if a person is a Christian simply by looking at him. But God has no problem identifying those who know Him. Those who are in the kingdom are obeying the King!

See also: Rom. 8:19, 2 Tim. 2:19

August 20
Read Luke 17:28-37

"Remember Lot's wife" v. 32

The morning God destroyed Sodom and Gomorrah, He sent two angels to rescue Lot and his family. Lot's wife looked back and she was turned into a pillar of salt (Genesis 19:26). Her life was lost even though the angels of God were leading her by the hand. Today, there is a stone pillar by the Dead Sea that is known as 'Lot's Wife'. If you go to Israel, your tour guide will point it out to you.

Lot is the picture of a carnal Christian who had his eyes on the treasures and pleasures of this world. As a result, he lost everything — even his wife! This is the plight of everyone who has his hope in the things of this world.

At times God may grant that certain people have angelic visitations or supernatural workings of God. But even these will not suffice if our hearts are in the wrong place. When the trumpet sounds and we are called in the twinkling of an eye, it will be too late to rearrange our priorities. "Now is the day of salvation" (2 Corinthians 6:2).

See also: Gen. 19:23-29, 2 Pet. 2:7-9

August 21
Read Luke 18:1-8

"Nevertheless, when the Son of Man comes, will He find faith on the earth?" v. 8

Jesus often asked questions as a method of teaching spiritual truth. Many times His questions were rhetorical and the answer was obvious to all. At other times He would sit down with His disciples and explain the answers in detail. But when Jesus asked the question of finding faith when He returned, apparently He Himself wasn't sure.

For twenty centuries, the Gospel has been communicated from one generation to the next. Now the torch is in our hands. To reach the next generation is of vital importance.

Will Christ find faith when He returns? I will say that if He returns while I am still living, He will! By God's grace, He will! What about you?

See also: 1 Kings 19:18, Heb. 10:36-39

August 22
Read Luke 18:9-14

"He also told this parable to those who trusted in themselves that they were righteous, and treated others with contempt" v. 9

Luke 18:9 is the best definition of a Pharisee that I can find— people who trust in themselves and despise others. Do you know someone like that? Watch out! Their disease is contagious. What a blight on the church they are!

We often divide people on the basis of wealth, or education, or race, or gender, or social standing. But Jesus divides people between those who trusted in Him and those who trusted in themselves. If I trust in myself, I see no value in Christ's work on my behalf. His sacrifice was not necessary for me. How arrogant can someone be to think such a thing!

Changing our trust from self to God is what is known as conversion. Is your trust in Christ and Christ alone?

See also: Acts 3:19, 1 Thess. 1:9, 1 Tim. 1:15

August 23
Read Luke 18:9-14

"God, be merciful to me, a sinner" v. 13

If there were but one attribute of God that we should be thankful for, it is His mercy. But mercy is more than just a feeling of pity toward someone in misery. True mercy not only feels compassion, but also possesses the ability to help someone in a time of need.

If someone were drowning and we stood helplessly on the shore unable to swim or help the victim, we would feel great remorse, but it would not be mercy. Mercy is the exercise of the ability to help someone. Mankind's greatest need is to be rescued from sin. God is extending His mercy to do that right now. What man needs to do is reach out and receive it.

PS. Some translations read, "God be merciful to me, <u>the</u> sinner". Personally recognizing our utter depravity is a prerequisite to finding His mercy.

See also: Ps. 23:6, Ps. 51:1, 1 Pet. 1:3

August 24
Read Matthew 19:3-9

"What therefore God has joined together, let not man separate" v. 6

The first and most important institution God has established is the family. A wedding is only one day. But a marriage is for a lifetime. Nevertheless, people spend more time preparing for the wedding than for their marriage.

Genesis 2:24 (which Jesus quoted) has three aspects: 1. Leave —The public legal ceremony recognized by the society, 2. Hold fast to — based on commitment love, not feeling love, and 3. One flesh — the physical aspect of marriage.

A problem in America today is that we get the order of events backward. The result is disrespect and mistrust which are great hindrances to the marriage relationship. We then run into problems which God wants us to avoid.

With so many divorces in our society, can we admit that we are doing something wrong? God was the original designer of marriage. Let us do things His way.

See also: Gen. 2:18-25, Heb. 13:4

August 25
Read Matthew 19:13-15

Let the little children come to Me and do not hinder them, for to such belongs the kingdom of Heaven. v. 14

"Would Jesus watch Charlie Brown?" That is the question I posed to my daughter when she wanted to watch the Christmas special.

Jesus came to be our Savior. He also came to be our teacher and our example. The question of what Jesus would do is a good one when determining the will of God for our lives. And certainly Jesus' teaching and example are good to follow when it comes to our attitude toward children.

But what about Charlie Brown? Would Jesus watch it on television? My daughter said He would. And I think He would too—with any four-year-old who would climb up in His lap and watch it with Him.

See also: Ps. 68:5, Mal. 2:15, Col. 3:21

August 26
Read Mark 10:13-16

"Let the children come to me; do not hinder them, for to such belongs the kingdom of God" v. 14

After returning from a preaching engagement, D.L. Moody reported that five and one-half people got saved. "Do you mean five adults and one child?" a friend asked. "No", said the great preacher, " Five children and one adult".

Mr. Moody knew if an adult is saved, his soul is secure for eternity, but a good portion of his earthly life has already passed. But if a child is saved, not only is his soul secure, but his entire life can be used for God's purposes.

Perhaps there is a child in your family that you can point toward the Savior. In doing so, you will not only be instrumental in redeeming a soul, but also a life.

See also: Ps. 127:3, Prov. 22:6, Eph. 6:4

August 27
Read Matthew 19:16-22

"If you would enter life, keep the commandments" v. 17

When asked about the moral standard to attain to, Jesus made reference to the Ten Commandments.

The original tablets of stone were not chiseled by the hand of Moses, but by the finger of God (Exodus 31:18). This is the only portion of Scripture that God personally wrote. The first set was broken at Mt. Sinai when Moses saw the idolatry of the Israelites. Moses received a second set that was lost during the Babylonian captivity.

It could be that these tablets of stone still exist today — one at the base of Mt. Sinai, and the other possibly under the rubble in Jerusalem. Perhaps as the end of the age approaches and lawlessness increases, these tablets will be found and the stones will again cry out to all mankind the holy standard of God's law by which we will be judged.

See also: Ex. 20:1-17, Rom. 13:8-10

August 28
Read Mark 10:17-22

"Jesus…said to him, 'You lack one thing: go, sell all that you have and give to the poor, and you will have treasure in heaven; and come follow me'" v. 21

A temporal value system rather than an eternal value system is a big problem with many people. As far as our eternal souls are concerned, earthly wealth is more of a liability than an asset. Jesus wanted the rich man to transfer his wealth from earth to heaven. His words to the rich man were, "Go…sell…give…and you will have…" The rich man's problem was not that he had riches but that riches had him. If he had done what Jesus told him, he would still have his riches. The only difference is they would have been in an account in heaven instead of on earth. He was as precarious as a drowning man trying to swim to shore with a bag of gold in each hand.

Where is your treasure?

See also: Ps. 19:10, Js. 2:5, Rev. 3:17-19

August 29
Read Mark 10:23-31

"It is easier for a camel to go through the eye of a needle than for a rich person to enter the kingdom of God" v. 25

The rich man did many things that were right:

1. He came to the right person — Jesus. No one in all of history has had the words of eternal life except Him.
2. He came with the right attitude — He ran and knelt, implying enthusiasm and reverence.
3. He asked the right question — "What must I do to inherit eternal life?" There is no more important question on earth to ask than that.
4. He got the right answer — Jesus put his finger on the one thing that was more important to him than God — his money.

Right person; Right attitude; Right question; Right answer; But wrong response. His name probably was well known in his community. But his name is not mentioned in the Scriptures. Even more sadly, it will not be mentioned in Heaven.

See also: Eccl. 5:10, Col. 3:5, 1 Tim. 6:6-10

August 30
Read Luke 18:18-30

"Jesus, seeing that he had become sad, said, 'How difficult it is for those who have wealth to enter the kingdom of God!'" v. 24

It is interesting to compare the rich ruler in chapter 18 with Zacchaeus in chapter 19. A wrong attitude toward money can have dire consequences. A right attitude can produce wonderful results.

>Money can buy: A house but not a home,
>   Food but not an appetite,
>   A bed but not sleep,
>   Books but not brains,
>   Amusements but not happiness,
>   Companions but not friends,
>   Loyalty but not love,
>   A crucifix but not a Savior,
>   A church but not Heaven.   (Copied)

See also: Deut. 6:10-12, Heb. 13:5

August 31
Read Matthew 19:16-22

"When the young man heard this he went away sorrowful, for he had great possessions" v. 22

We are saved by the merits of Christ, not by works. But our hearts need to be in the proper state if we are going to receive His merits. In the case of the rich young ruler, there was something more important to him than a relationship with God —his money. Thus, he was an idolater.

When the young man turned and walked away, Jesus didn't say, "Wait, I was too hard on you." Our Lord knew there was simply no way an idolater could enter God's kingdom. Though he was a highly moral man, keeping God's commandments, his heart was fixed on his money rather than on God.

Money has no merit in the Kingdom of God. Be not deceived into thinking otherwise.

See also: Deut. 8:11-14, Jer. 9:23-24, Rev. 3:17

September 1
Read Luke 18:31-34

"They understood none of these things" v. 34

An ant crawling across a newspaper knows nothing of what is written on it. The words and concepts are incomprehensible to it. The same thing was true of Jesus' disciples when He first told them of God's plan of redemption. With many today this is still true.

The meaning of Jesus' death and resurrection on our behalf can only be understood by Divine revelation — by the Spirit of God witnessing to our spirit. Only then can the life-changing message of Calvary perform its work in our hearts.

God giving His Word to us through the prophets and apostles is called 'inspiration'. God giving us understanding of what it means as we read it is called 'illumination'. Each time you open the Bible, ask God to give you a heart that can understand the beautiful things written therein.

See also: Ps. 119:18, Lk. 24:45, 1 Cor. 2:14-16, 1 Jn. 2:20, 1 Jn. 5:20

September 2
Read Mark 10:35-45

"For even the Son of Man came not to be served but to serve, and to give His life as a ransom for many" v. 45 [June Memory Verse]

The book of Mark presents Jesus as a servant. Mark 10:45 is the key verse of this gospel. Serving and giving are the two chief attributes Jesus ascribes to Himself.

Mark (often called John Mark) was not always a good servant. In Acts 13:13 he quit the missionary tour and went home. On the next missionary journey, Paul refused to take Mark along (Acts 15:36-38). As he matured, however, he learned what it meant to be a servant. In 2 Timothy 4:11 (the last letter Paul wrote) he said, "Get Mark and bring him with you, for he is very useful to me for ministry."

Mark, who was not a servant, later learned what it means to serve and was then used by God to present his Savior as a servant in his gospel. Serving and giving—are those the attributes that describe your life? Let us pursue a life of servanthood, that we may be more like our Savior.

See also: Gal. 5:13, 1 Pet. 4:10

September 3
Read Luke 18:35-43

"He cried out all the more, 'Son of David, have mercy on me'" v. 39

"I prayed to God for help but He didn't answer. I guess it wasn't God's will to heal me." If Bartimaeus had that attitude, he would have never called out to Jesus a second time.

The Lord is not reluctant to answer our prayers. His delays are not his denials. Rather, His delays are designed to strengthen our faith.

Do you have a long term need that has not yet been met? Genuinely cry out to God again. Remember, however, that you will never get a million dollar answer to a ten cent prayer.

See also: Heb. 5:7, 1 Jn. 5:14-15

September 4
Read Matthew 20:29-34

"What do you want me to do for you?" v. 32

These blind men had called out for mercy several times. But how did they want that mercy to be expressed? By receiving their sight, naturally. The Lord fulfilled their request as soon as it was specific enough to be answered.

I can't think of one time in the Gospels when a prayer to Jesus was more than one sentence long. But there may be times in our lives when we pray long prayers, and when we are through, God would say, "Now just what was it that you wanted Me to do?" A specific short appeal on the basis of mercy is the prayer He always answers.

See also: 1 Sam. 1:12-18, 1 Jn. 5:15

September 5
Read Mark 10:46-52

"As He was leaving Jericho …Bartimaeus, a blind beggar…was sitting by the roadside" v. 46

Jesus was passing through Jericho. He would never pass that way again. Bartimaeus would never in his life have this opportunity again. If he didn't take advantage of it when he did, he would have languished for the remainder of his miserable life as a blind beggar. But he called out at the right time, to the right person, with the right request. The Lord heard and responded. The man was healed.

There comes a time in every person's life when the Lord is passing by for the last time. There will be no more tomorrows—no more next times. Today is the only day we have to get right with God. Make your decision and call on Him right now. He will show you His mercy just as He did to Bartimaeus.

See also: Ps. 6:9, 2 Cor. 6:2

September 6
Read Luke 19:1-10

"Behold, Lord, the half of my goods I give to the poor. And if I have defrauded anyone of anything, I restore it fourfold" v. 8

It is said that a carnal person loves money and uses people while a righteous person loves people and uses money. An idol is anything we love or trust more than God. One of the biggest idols of our nation is money. Anyone who loves their money more than their Maker is in big trouble. We are called in Scripture to renounce this idol.

Generosity is a virtue highly valued in the Kingdom of God. We can tell that a person has genuinely been converted when, like Zacchaeus, a stealer becomes a giver.

See also: 2 Cor. 9:7, Eph. 4:28, Heb. 13:5

September 7
Read Luke 19:1-10

"Jesus said to him, 'Today salvation has come to this house'" v. 9

There are five days that wrought our salvation. The <u>first</u> was a day in eternity past when God in His providence looked down through history and chose you (Ephesians 1:4). <u>Second</u> was the day Jesus rose from the dead to give us new life (Ephesians 1:20). <u>Third</u> was the day you personally applied God's provision by trusting in Him (John 1:12). <u>Fourth</u> is today, as you live out your salvation moment by moment (Philippians 2:12-13). And <u>fifth</u> is the day in the future when we receive our new bodies and are made perfect in Him (2 Corinthians 5:1).

Wow! Salvation means a lot!

See also: Acts 4:12, Rom. 13:11

September 8
Read Luke 19:1-10

"For the Son of Man came to seek and to save the lost" v. 10 [August Memory Verse]

Luke 19:10 is the key verse of Luke. Memorize it. God's quest for man began in the Garden of Eden when He called out to Adam, "Where are you?" (Genesis 3:9). Since that day He has been seeking and wooing every person to Himself. He is still seeking the person that we have long ago given up on. He is also seeking you!

It is quite ironic that the God of the universe is seeking man while most of mankind is hiding from Him just as our father Adam did. He is not reluctant to save us, but actively concerned.

In Luke 19:3, we read that Zacchaeus "was seeking to see who Jesus was". We have His promise that if we seek Him we will find Him (Mt. 7:7-8). That was true of Zacchaeus. It can be true of you as well. As He seeks us, we need to continue seeking Him.

See also: Is. 55:6, Jer. 29:12-13, 2 Pet. 3:9

September 9
Read Luke 19:28-44

"I tell you, if these were silent, the very stones would cry out" v. 40

Although the nation of Israel was given overwhelming evidence of who Jesus was, they still refused to believe. They tried to silence Him by having Him crucified. A few years later, they tried to silence His followers by driving them out of Jerusalem. Christianity was effectively banished from the city (Acts 8:1).

In 70 AD the Roman soldier Titus captured Jerusalem. One of his exploits was to turn over all the stones of the temple, fulfilling Jesus' prophecy of Luke 19:44. The believers were silenced and the rocks by being turned over spoke! Either with us or without us, God will be glorified. Let us be "living stones", as it says in 1 Peter 2:5, giving praise to the One who will use even rocks if we don't speak. If God spoke through stones, can't He speak through you?

See also: Ps. 150:6, Acts 8:4, 1 Pet. 2:4-5

September 10
Read Mark 11:20-26

"Whenever you stand praying, forgive if you have anything against anyone, so that your Father also who is in Heaven may forgive you your trespasses" v. 25

This verse in the context of prayer is not an afterthought or misplaced. The two things that hinder our prayers are unconfessed sin on our part, and unforgiven sin, also on our part. Failing to confess or failing to forgive clutters up our prayer life. The offending person may even be no longer living, but what he has done can still influence your life.

Forgiveness does not in any way say the offender was right. That person probably was very wrong. Some would say, "But how can I forgive and forget? I'll remember the evil done to me as long as I live." Yes, we will remember historically, but we are to forget it emotionally. Place the offender in the hands of God who always judges justly. Forgiveness may not change the other person. But it will bring healing to your soul; then that person will no longer have control of your life. Forgiveness does not change the past. But it certainly can change the future.

See also: Rom. 12:16-21, Eph. 4:32, 1 Pet. 3:7

September 11
Read Matthew 22:1-14
"For many are called, but few are chosen" v. 14

Who are those that Jesus classified as the chosen? Is there a special group of elite people that God has predestined to find favor in His sight while the rest of the world struggles and perishes?

The <u>called</u> ones are all the people of the world who hear the message of Christ. The <u>chosen</u> are those who respond to His call. The reason there are only a few chosen is because only a few take heed to God's voice. The answer as to whether you are one of God's chosen lies not with God but with you. He has given the invitation to 'whoever will' to come to Him and find life. What is your response?

The hymn writer, Philip Bliss put it this way:

Whosoever cometh need not delay,

Now the door is open, enter while you may;

Jesus is the true, the only Living Way;

Whosoever will may come.

See also: Rom. 10:13, Rom. 10:18, 1 Pet. 2:9, Rev. 22:17

September 12
Read John 12:20-26
"Sir, we wish to see Jesus" v. 21

"Where is Jesus?" I asked my three year old daughter. I was expecting her to either say, "In my heart", or "In Heaven". But her answer surprised me. In reference to her Children's Bible, she said, "He's in the Book."

There is no substitute for a first-hand look at Jesus. The Greeks were not content with seeing Philip or Andrew. They wanted to see Jesus Himself. And where do we look today if we want to see Jesus as He really is? In the Book! The Bible is God's special revelation of Himself. If you wish to see Jesus, follow a child's example and look in the Book!

See also: Josh. 1:8, Acts 17:11

September 13
Read John 12:20-26
"Sir, we wish to see Jesus" v. 21

This little phrase (from which this book got its title) deserves another day of thought: Visualize a picture of John 3:16 written in artistically crafted calligraphy and shaded skillfully to make each word and phrase stand out in a beautiful way. Then imagine pulling back a distance from the writing, and seeing the face of Jesus.

The Bible is made up of little black symbols called letters. They are put together to form words, and then sentences and thoughts. But if you stand back a little and take a broad view, you see the face of our Savior.

There are many distorted views of Jesus in our world today. But if you want to know Him as He really is, read your Bible. As you read day after day, like putting together the pieces of a puzzle, you will begin to see His face. The best picture of Jesus you will see on this side of eternity is in the Bible. If you make it your daily prayer to see Jesus in the Bible, people will also see Him in you!

See also: Heb. 2:9, Rev. 1:7

September 14
Read Matthew 22:15-22
Then the Pharisees went and plotted how to entangle Him in His words. And they sent their disciples to Him along with the Herodians" v. 15-16

The Pharisees and Herodians were mortal enemies. The Pharisees were religious people who wanted Roman rule removed from their country. The Herodians were a political party in favor of Roman rule. The only thing that they agreed upon was their opposition to Jesus.

If opposition to Jesus united His enemies, shouldn't commitment to Him unite His followers? Isn't it about time that Jesus' disciples discovered that they are all saved by the same Lord and have the same Spirit?

Because Christ is above all earthly controversy, He could take Simon, a Jewish zealot, and Matthew, a tax collector, and unite them under His lordship.

Let us not look at the differences we may have with fellow believers. Rather, let us pursue a path of oneness in Christ regardless of our political and cultural differences.

See also: 1 Cor. 1:12-13, Gal. 3:26-29, Eph. 4:1-3

September 15
Read Mark 12:13-17

"Render to Caesar the things that are Caesar's, and to God the things that are God's" v. 17

I work for the IRS. I work and earn money. Then the IRS takes it!

Whose image is on the denarius? Caesar's. And what has God's image on it? Answer: You! And your children! You were created in the image of God. Therefore, you belong to God. Caesar just might end up getting our money, our land, our possessions. But God has laid claim to our hearts. Therefore, give your heart without reservation to God. I promise you will not regret it.

Give of your best to the Master; Naught else is worthy His love;

He gave Himself as your ransom, Gave up His glory above;

Laid down His life without murmur, you from sin's ruin to save;

Give Him your heart's adoration, Give Him the best that you have.

(Copied)

See also: Gen. 1:27, Rom. 13:7

September 16
Read Mark 12:28-34

"The second is like this: 'You shall love your neighbor as yourself'" v. 31

All of the "Do not's" in the Bible are superseded by one big "Do" — the command to love! It is the number one law of the kingdom of God. What greater standard could we attain to than to love others as our own souls?

When I was in Vietnam I had a great struggle with this command. How could I love my fellow soldiers who every day, every hour cursed my Lord? From their first breath in the morning to their last words at night they uttered curses. I complained to the Lord about my inability to love them. Then in my spirit, God answered, "I never expected you to love them. I want to love them through you."

What a relief to know that God's command to love also brings with it His power to carry it out! I discovered that God's love was not a standard to attain to but a resource to draw from!

See also: Rom. 13:8-10, Gal. 5:15, Js. 2:8

September 17
Read Matthew 23:13-36

"Woe to you, scribes and Pharisees, hypocrites!" v. 13

Jesus began His public ministry with blessings (Mt. 5:1-12). He ended His ministry with seven woes! God wants to bless us. He wants to forgive. He wants to restore us. He wants us to follow His ways and live. That was His purpose in coming to earth.

Abraham Lincoln was asked if God was on the side of the Union or the side of the Confederacy. His answer was very profound — "Sir, my concern is not whether God is on our side; my greatest concern is to be on God's side, for God is always right." For those who refuse His ways and reject His blessings, there is only judgment ahead. Woes are coming upon the whole earth (Rev. 8:13). Be sure you are on the right side!

See also: Is.30:1, Ezek. 18:21, Joel 2:1-3, Rev. 6:16-17

September 18
Read Matthew 23:25-28

"So you also outwardly appear righteous to others, but within you are full of hypocrisy and lawlessness" v. 28

The experienced woodsman looked at the stately oak and said, "That tree is no good." He pointed out a place high on the trunk where a branch had died many years ago and rotted away. Then he pointed to a hole in the base of the tree.

I took my chain saw and started cutting. In only a few seconds, the tree was on the ground. And sure enough, it was hollow! Only a few inches around the outside of the tree were good. The inside had all rotted away. If I had not cut it, the next strong wind could have blown it down.

How many people are like that stately oak? They look good on the outside, but have no spiritual substance on the inside. Let us fortify our hearts with love and truth so we may be healthy and strong in the center of our beings.

See also: 1 Sam. 16:7, Eph. 3:16

September 19
Read Matthew 23:29-36

"Truly, I say to you, all these things will come upon this generation" v. 36

The more light we are given, the more responsibility we are given to obey it. The same generation that saw the mighty miracles of God also saw His judgment. To see the hand of God at work in our midst and turn away from it is what the Bible calls "hardening your heart" (Hebrews 3:7-8, 15, 4:7). This is a very dangerous thing to do.

God is very reluctant to pass judgment on anyone. He does not pronounce woes out of a heart of vengeance. He takes no pleasure in the death and destruction of the wicked (Ezekiel 33:11). The fact simply is that when His grace is refused, only His hot justice remains.

See also: Ezek. 18:24, Heb. 10:26-31, 2 Pet. 2:21

September 20
Read Luke 21:5-9

"As for these things that you see, the days will come when there will not be left here one stone upon another that will not be thrown down" v. 6

The city of Pompeii was destroyed when Mt. Vesuvius erupted in 79 AD. While excavating the sight, archeologists came across an inscription on a wall which read, "Nothing in the world can endure forever". What a fitting prophecy for that great city!

I recall traveling on I-94 into St. Paul. As I viewed the massive buildings, Hebrews 13:14 came to mind, which says, "Here we have no lasting city." I was overwhelmed with the thought that someday those massive buildings will only be piles of rubble.

We certainly should be investing more in eternity and not build monuments to ourselves down here.

See also: Heb. 12:26-27, Heb. 13:14

September 21
Read Matthew 24:1-3

"As He sat on the Mount of Olives, the disciples came to Him privately, saying, 'Tell us, when will these things be, and what will be the sign of Your coming, and the close of the age?'" v. 3

Matthew 24:1 through Matthew 25:46 is what is known as the "Olivet Discourse". If you want to know about the end of the age (not the end of the earth, but the end of the age) this is the place to start.

Jesus gave this discourse on the Wednesday afternoon before His crucifixion. He and His disciples were on the Mount of Olives where they camped out at night. As they looked west across the Kidron Valley they could see the wall of Jerusalem and the Eastern Gate, where He rode into the city on a donkey the previous Sunday. The Eastern Gate is the same gate He will enter again when He returns. It is the most important piece of real estate in the world! What a setting to hear about the end of the age and His coming again! The olive trees there are some 3000 years old and the same trees that were there when Jesus gave this discourse. Oh, if those trees could talk!

See also: Zech. 14:4

September 22
Read Matthew 24:1-8

"See that no one leads you astray. For many will come in my name, saying, 'I am the Christ', and they will lead many astray" v. 4-5

Bankers tell us that when they train bank tellers how to spot counterfeit money, they always use real money, not the counterfeit. It is not necessary for us to know and understand every error or false teaching that comes along. All we need to know is the truth. Then, falsehood will be obvious to us.

When Jesus was asked about the end times, the first words from His lips were that many would be deceived. As people turn from truth, they naturally turn to error (2 Timothy 4:4). Let us be so resolutely committed to truth that error would have no appeal to us.

See also: 2 Tim. 3:13-14, 2 Tim. 4:1-5

September 23
Read Luke 21:25-28

"People fainting with fear and with foreboding of what is coming on the world" v. 26

It has been said that there are three kinds of people in the world: Those living in fear; those too ignorant to fear; and those who know their Bible. It has also been said that there are 365 'fear not's' in the Bible — one for every day of the year!

Trust and fear cannot live in the same house. When fear walks in the front door, faith sneaks out the back door. (The opposite is also true.) One must dominate. When trust dominates, the fruit is peace. When fear dominates, the fruit is worry. Our job is to make God totally responsible for us by giving Him complete control of our lives.

When fear knocks, send faith to the door!

See also: Is. 41:10, Heb. 13:6, 1 Jn. 4:18

September 24
Read Mark 13:1-8

"And when you hear of wars and rumors of wars, do not be alarmed. This must take place, but the end is not yet" v. 7

This verse gave me great peace when I was in Vietnam, and still gives me peace to this day when I hear of violence and bloodshed around the world.

In Vietnam, during the Tet offensive when every American base was simultaneously attacked in one night, I remember seeing plane after plane fly over our heads, strafing enemy positions. Tracers, flares and bombs lit up the night sky. Turning around to see where the American planes were coming from, I saw nothing but the beautiful, starlit, tropical night sky. How beautiful it was! What a contrast between the workings of man and the workings of God! Feeling such peace, I went into the bunker and promptly fell asleep. When I awoke, the skirmish was over. I was both thankful that I was alive and regretting that God hadn't taken me to be with Him that night. Whichever it would have been, there was God's peace living in my heart.

Oh the rumors! Oh the workings of evil men on the earth! But in the midst of it, you can have God's personal peace. Amen!

See also: Is. 26:3, Phil. 4:6-7, Col. 3:15

September 25
Read Matthew 24:3-14

"And this gospel of the kingdom will be proclaimed throughout the whole world as a testimony to all nations, and then the end will come" v. 14

Dr. Albert Simpson, missionary statesman of a century ago, was approached by a reporter from the New York Journal. "Do you know when the Lord will return?" the reporter asked Simpson. To the reporter's surprise, Simpson said he knew the exact day of Christ's coming. Simpson opened his Bible and read Matthew 24:14.

Is Jesus going to return? Absolutely! When? When the last person on earth has an opportunity to respond to His mercy and grace. For the first time in the history of the earth, this generation has the potential to fulfill Matthew 24:14 and bring about the personal return of Christ to earth! That gives His people great incentive to hasten His coming by spreading the gospel in every way possible.

Imagine if you were to lead someone to Christ on the very day of His return!

See also: Acts 1:8, 2 Pet. 3:11-12, Rev. 14:15-16

September 26
Read Matthew 24:23-28

"For false christs and false prophets will arise and perform great signs and wonders, so as to lead astray, if possible, even the elect" v. 24

Generations ago, people had a fool-proof way of leading sheep to slaughter. They had what was called a 'Judas goat' which the sheep would mindlessly follow down a corridor which led to their death. The one they were following was leading them to slaughter and they didn't even know it!

Jesus referred to people as sheep without a shepherd (Matthew 9:36). The next time you are in a crowd, just observe people and see how true that is. It is very easy to lead an unthinking person any place you want him to go.

An antichrist is someone who tries to take the place of the true Christ. Even though they may show many signs and wonders, they still lead people astray and eventually to death. Just because someone poses as a leader doesn't mean he is leading people in the right direction.

Mark this well: Just because you see a sign doesn't mean it is from God.

See also: Deut. 13:1-3, Acts 20:28-31, 2 Thess. 2:9-12, 1 Jn. 2:18-19

September 27
Read Matthew 24:32-35

"Heaven and earth will pass away, but My words will not pass away" v. 35

When I was in the military, I knew an agnostic who claimed that the Bible was not true. I asked him, "If it isn't true and we get to the end of life what have I lost?" His answer —"Nothing." Then I asked him, "If it is true and we get to the end of life, what have you lost?" He stood there speechless, for he knew that he would be lost forever.

I am convinced that Jesus' words are 100% true. But let's suppose that they are only 50% reliable. Let's go one step further and say Jesus was only 10% factual in what He said. If there were only one chance in ten that Jesus was accurate in what He said about life and death, Heaven and hell, salvation and damnation, the wisest thing we could do is make Him our Savior and obey Him as Lord.

See also: Ps. 19:7-11, Is. 40:8, 2 Pet. 1:20-21

September 28
Read Matthew 24:36-44

"But concerning that day and hour no one knows, not even the angels of Heaven, nor the Son, but the Father only" v. 36

Some people desire to set dates and tell us the day Christ will return. But for them to do so is to assume that they have more knowledge than Christ Himself!

We have the blessed hope of His return but there are things in this world that are more important than knowing the exact day of His coming. Our chief concern is to spread His gospel throughout the world. That is God's number one priority for us in this age.

Should we anticipate His return? Yes. Should we be alert? Absolutely. Should we be ready? Most certainly. Should we set dates? No.

See also: Acts 1:7, 1 Thess. 5:1-6, 2 Pet. 3:9-13

September 29
Read Matthew 24:36-44

"They were unaware until the flood came and swept them all away, so will be the coming of the Son of Man" v. 39

Noah spent 120 years building the ark. It was longer than a football field including the goal posts on each end. No doubt thousands watched him build it. Perhaps some of them even helped him. Yet they did not know that judgment was coming. They didn't see the 300 cubit long sign that God was giving them.

Year after year, Noah and his sons worked on the ark. Finally it was completed. The animals were brought in. I'm guessing that the people were all partying as they watched the animals being loaded (v. 38). Then Noah and his family got on board. Gen. 7:16 says, "The Lord shut him in." The closed door meant safety for Noah and his family, but it meant no more opportunity for those outside. Only destruction and death lay ahead for them.

I can imagine people and animals on every high hill as the water came up. The high hills would keep getting smaller and smaller as people crowded closer and closer together to stay out of the water just a bit longer. Finally the little islands and their inhabitants would disappear beneath the waves.

"As it was… so shall it be." Be ready!

See also: Gen. 6:11-18, Heb. 11:7

September 30
Read Mark 13:24-31

"Heaven and earth will pass away, but my words will not pass away" v. 31

The origin of the Bible is unique to any other book. 2 Tim. 3:16 says, "All scripture is breathed out by God…" Its duration is also unique in that Jesus said it will last longer than the very earth on which we walk!

If a survey were taken and a certain percent of the people thought the Bible was the authoritative word of God and a certain percent did not, that would not change a thing. The Scriptures are true and reliable whether people believe them or not. The opinion of man is not needed to substantiate what God has said.

If the Bible indeed is what it claims to be, then we should study it daily, not only that we may master its truths, but that its truths may master us.

See also: Is. 40:8, 2 Tim. 3:16, 2 Pet. 1:20-21

October 1
Read Matthew 24:36-44

"Therefore, stay awake, for you do not know on what day your Lord is coming" v. 42

The most important day in the history of mankind is still to come — the day when Jesus returns to set up His kingdom on earth. The Bible refers to it as 'that day' (v. 36). He will then settle the accounts of every individual; and the destiny of every person will be eternally sealed.

Next to 'that day', the most important day is 'this day' — today. The only real time we have is now. It is what we do with our todays that will affect our outcome on 'that day'.

This age will not end with mankind annihilating itself, but with the return of Jesus Christ. Jesus didn't say to be concerned about persecutions or wars or even the antichrist. Our chief concern is to be ready when He returns. Let's live each day in the light of 'that day'.

See also: Amos 5:18-20, Zeph. 1:14-16, 2 Tim. 1:12, 2 Tim. 4:8, 2 Pet. 3:10-11

October 2
Read Mark 13:28-37

"Therefore stay awake — for you do not know when the Master of the house will come, in the evening, or at midnight, or when the rooster crows, or in the morning" v. 35

"Minutemen": The word still inspires pride in our hearts today. They were the Massachusetts militia who were prepared at a minute's notice, day or night, to make a stand against the British. With everything from gun powder to water, they were ready to go. Never did they go to bed at night without their boots being ready for running feet! That is how God expects us to be as the end of the age approaches — even 'in the twinkling of an eye'! (1 Corinthians 15:52)

Mark 13:35 tells us we do not know something — the exact time of His coming. But verse 29 tells us something we can know — that the time is near. We cannot know the day or hour. But we can know the season. Do you have the spirit of a Minuteman?

See also: Dan. 12:2, 1 Thess. 3:13, 1 Thess. 4:15-18

October 3
Read Matthew 25:1-13

"Five of them were foolish, and five were wise. For when the foolish took their lamps, they took no oil with them" v. 2-3

All ten of the virgins thought the bridegroom would return as he said. All ten made preparations. But only five were ready when he finally came. If the same ratio is true when Jesus returns, only half of those who say they believe He is coming will be ready. Only half of the church will be prepared to welcome Him.

The distinction between the wise and the foolish is not about how many details we know about His return. It is about being truly prepared to meet Him. His return could very well be during your lifetime. Are you ready? Really ready?

See also: 1 Cor. 15:51-54, 1 Thess. 1:9-10

October 4
Read Matthew 25:1-13

"Watch therefore, for you know neither the day nor the hour" v. 13

In Jewish tradition, the bridegroom went and made a binding agreement to marry his bride. It was much more binding than American engagements. He then went home and built a house in preparation for his bride. (This is what Joseph was doing when he found out Mary was pregnant.) When the house was complete, he went to claim his bride. The bride and her companions never knew the day, nor hour, the bridegroom would come. They were to be continuously ready. The same is true with the church as we await the return of our Groom, the Lord Jesus Christ. His return is closer today than it was yesterday! Let's be ready.

See also: 1 Thess. 5:1-11, 2 Pet. 3:10-12, Rev. 19:7

October 5
Read Matthew 25:31-40

"Truly I say to you, as much as you did it to one of the least of these my brothers, you did it to me" v. 40

"Why, Lord," said the man. "Why are you so indifferent to that poor little girl sitting in the cold? Surely You are able. But, God, You seem so indifferent to her plight. What kind of a God are you who doesn't care for Your creatures?"

As usual, God was silent, so the man went home. That night as the man laid his head on his pillow, he again thought of the little girl. But this time, an answer came to him — "I care very much for that little girl, my son. That is why I sent you to her. I even arranged your day to meet her and see her and help her. But you did nothing."

In shame and fear, the man realized it was not God, but him who was distant and uncaring. From that day on, he became a vessel of God to help others.

"Lord, help us to take advantage of the opportunities you put before us to be Your hands and feet and heart. Amen."

See also: Js. 2:14-17, 1 Jn. 3:17, 1 Jn. 4:20

October 6
Read Matthew 25:41:46

"Then He will say to those on His left, 'Depart from me, you cursed, into the eternal fire prepared for the devil and his angels'" v. 41

Compare Matthew 25:34 with Matthew 25:41. One says come; the other says depart. One says a kingdom is prepared; the other says eternal fire is prepared. What a contrast! Please note also that the eternal fire was not prepared for people, but for the devil and his angels.

I have heard people particularly from African cultures who base their theology not only on what they believe, but also on what they do. Both the believing and the doing of the Gospel need to come together. Jesus makes it clear here that our status in eternity will be based on what we do on earth. True faith always is translated into faithfulness.

See also: Rom. 1:14, 2 Thess. 1:8, Js. 1:22, 1 Pet. 4:17

October 7
Read John 12:1-8

"Mary therefore took a pound of expensive ointment made from pure nard, and anointed the feet of Jesus and wiped His feet with her hair" v. 3

Every time we see Mary, she is in the same place— at the feet of Jesus. The first time was for <u>instruction</u> (Luke 10:38-39). The second time was for <u>comfort</u> (John 11:32). This time, she is at His feet for <u>worship</u>.

Worship means to show worth to. When we worship and express to Him how valuable He is to us, inevitably someone will protest and say what we are doing is a waste. That is what Judas did. But Jesus defended Mary's actions. Her sacrifice was not a waste in God's eyes.

The result of Mary's worship was, "The house was filled with the fragrance of the perfume." Everyone around her sensed the fragrance of her worship. Let's honor Him in such a way that those around us may realize the beauty of our worship as well.

See also: Ps. 29:2, Micah 6:7-8, Phil. 4:18

October 8
Read John 13:1-11

"Then He poured water into a basin and began to wash the disciples' feet" v. 5

Throughout the Gospels, we see people coming to Jesus' feet for various reasons: for healing, for comfort, for teaching, for worship, etc. But in our text today, we see Jesus coming to our feet.

There are times in our lives when there is no place to go except to the feet of Jesus. But for cleansing from the defilement of the world, Jesus comes to our feet. If we protest, like Peter, our Lord's response to us will also be, "If I do not wash you, you have no share with Me" (v. 8).

What an amazing thing that the King of Glory, before whom every creature in the universe will bow, comes before our feet and does something that no one else can do —He cleanses us! From there, let us follow His example by going and washing the feet of others.

See also: Ps. 51:2, Eph. 5:26-27, Heb. 10:22

October 9
Read John 13:12-20

"For I have given you an example, that you also should do just as I have done to you" v. 15

Jesus is more than an example. He is our Creator, our Lord, our Savior, the Alpha and Omega, and we could give a hundred other words to describe Him. But He is our example as well. And He called us to follow His example particularly in serving others.

The old adage, "Don't follow me, follow Jesus" is not fully biblical. We are examples either for good or for bad whether we want to be or not.

Another adage of a decade ago, "What Would Jesus Do?" is still a good one to follow. The Apostle Paul certainly followed the example of Christ in his lifestyle. Then he asked his converts to follow his example as well as them becoming examples to others. And the cycle goes on and on from one generation to the next. I can name countless saints who have been wonderful examples to me. I am thankful to God for them. And now God has raised you up to be an example to still others. I ask you to take your responsibility seriously.

See also: Phil. 3:17, 1 Thess. 1:7, 1 Tim. 4:12, Tit. 2:7-8

October 10
Read John 13:21-30

"One of His disciples, whom Jesus loved, was reclining at table close to Jesus" v. 23

I am so glad that God loves us all differently. (This is not a misprint — God loves each of us differently!) He does not have a cookie-cutter, one-size-fits-all love for the general population. He made each of us uniquely different. No two of us are the same. Likewise, He has a unique, one-of-a-kind love for each of us — and that includes you personally. His love for you is like His love for no one else in the universe. You are very special in His eyes!

There are also different categories of love for each of us. Hosea 14:4 says <u>free love</u>. John 15:13 tells of <u>great love</u>. 1 John 4:18 mentions <u>perfect love</u>. The true depth of His love is only limited by our capacity to receive it. As we return that love to Him and give it to our fellow man, let us remember that God's love is not a standard to attain to, but a resource to draw from.

See also: 1 Cor. 13:1-13, 1 Jn. 4:7-12

October 11
Read Luke 22:14-20

"This is my body, which is given for you…This cup that is poured out for you is the new covenant in My blood" v. 19-20

2 Peter 1:4 says that we are "Partakers of the divine nature." Holy Communion is a graphic illustration of that fact. When we partake of the bread and the wine, we are in essence ingesting Christ. We are illustrating in a physical way the spiritual reality of the necessity of Christ being within us in order for us to live the Christian life.

If you had communion last Sunday, its cost to you was very little. But for us to have the privilege to sit and partake of Holy Communion cost Jesus Christ His life. His holy body was broken. His divine blood was shed —our text says 'for you'. Partaking of communion is very costly to Christ.

The next time we have communion, let us remember its true cost. That will help us to partake in a worthy manner.

See also: 1 Cor. 11:23-26, 1 Pet. 1:18-19

October 12
Read Mark 14:27-31, 66-72

"And Jesus said to him, 'Truly, I tell you, this very night, before the rooster crows twice, you will deny Me three times'" v. 30

A psychic set up her booth in a large shopping mall and began peddling her predictions. One day a blind man made his way to her booth and asked, "Can you tell me where the toothpaste is?"

The psychic indignantly said she didn't work in the store and couldn't tell him where the tooth- paste was.

With all the conviction of a prophet, the blind man said, "If you can't tell me where the tooth- paste is, how can you tell me what is going to happen tomorrow!?"

What a contrast this psychic is with Jesus, who knew the hour of the morning the rooster would crow and the events that would precede it! In Peter's case, Jesus' prophecy wasn't very pleasant. Nevertheless, whatever circumstances we find ourselves in, we can be absolutely certain that He knows our future and will be there to see us through every obstacle we face.

See also: Ps. 139:1-12, Acts 27:22-25

October 13
Read Luke 22:31-34

"Behold, Satan demanded to have you, that he might sift you like wheat, but I have prayed for you" v. 31-32

Although we can't see it, the Bible tells of spiritual activity taking place around us. Satan is the prince of darkness. When considering his influence, there are two opposite errors people fall into. The first is to consider that he has no power or influence over us at all. The opposite error is to assume that he has all power and we are helpless victims of his attacks. Both extremes are not only wrong, but dangerous.

Looking at our text today, we find that the barrier erected between us and the evil one is prayer. Thank the Lord that the evil of the wicked one is repelled simply by praying.

Do you have a friend that Satan desires to "sift as wheat"? Stop right now and erect a barrier of prayer between your friend and the enemy of his soul.

See also: Gen. 19:29, Job 1:6-12, Js. 4:7

October 14
Read John 13:31-35

"A new commandment I give to you, that you love one another: just as I have loved you, you also are to love one another. By this all people will know that you are My disciples" v. 34 [September Memory Verse]

Every family has certain traits that are predominant. Some are tall while others are short. Some families are intellectual. Others are more athletic. Some are light skinned, while others are darker. The predominant trait of the family of God is love. This is how the world will recognize us as Christians.

The Old Covenant commands us to love one another as we love ourselves. The New Covenant commands us to love others as Christ loved us. That is why Jesus called it a 'new' commandment. His love is an inexhaustible resource.

See also: Lev. 19:18, Js. 2:8, 1 Jn. 4:7-11

October 15
Read John 13:36-38

"Simon Peter said to Him, 'Lord, where are you going?' v. 36

    Just after Jesus washed His disciple's feet He had an intimate conversation with them. How I wish I could have been there! Four of His disciples' questions are recorded for us in Holy Scripture:

    Peter's Question: <u>Destination</u> — "Where are You going?" (John 13:36)

    Thomas' Question: <u>Explanation</u> — "How can we know the way?" (John 14:5)

    Philip's Question: <u>Revelation</u> — "Show us the Father" (John 14:8)

    Judas' Question: <u>Manifestation</u> —"How will You show Yourself to us?" (Jn. 14: 22--paraphrased)

If Jesus were sitting before you, what questions would you ask Him? I know that many of our questions will never be answered on this side of eternity. And at times Jesus might say to us as did to the Twelve, "I have many things to say to you, but you cannot bear them now"(John 16:12). Many times, when I have a question, I simply ask the Lord. Though I have not often gotten an immediate answer, many times within a few days or weeks, I receive an answer through reading His Word or through listening to Christian radio. Just directly ask Him, and expect Him to answer as soon as you are able to receive the answer.

See also: 2 Pet. 3:18, 1 Jn. 5:20

October 16
Read John 13:31-36

"Where I am going you cannot follow Me now; but you shall follow Me later" v. 36

    Heaven is perfect, right? Wrong! For something to be perfect it must be complete in every way. There must not be one missing element. Everything must be in its proper place.
    Jesus went to prepare a place for you — that is for you personally! There will be one vacant mansion in Heaven and one missing seat at the Marriage Supper of the Lamb until you get there to occupy it! There is a place set for you with your name on it! Really! Heaven won't be perfect until you and I get there —along with millions of others, of course!

See also: Heb. 11-39-40, 1 Jn. 3:3, Rev. 19:7

October 17
Read John 14:1-4

"I go to prepare a place for you. And if I go and prepare a place for you, I will come again and will take you to myself, that where I am you may be also" v. 2-3

This verse is a promise of a groom to His bride. We are His bride. As He is preparing a place for us, we need to be preparing for that place.

It took God only six days to create the heavens and the earth and the sea and the sky and the depths of the earth and all living creatures great and small. Wow! But for the last 2000 years He has been preparing a place for us. How great it must be! Someone has said if God is preparing a place for us, we must send up the materials beforehand. If that is so, how large will your place be?

See also: 1 Cor. 3:12-15, Rev. 22:20

October 18
Read John 14:4-6

"Jesus said to him, 'I am the way, and the truth, and the life. No one comes to the Father except through Me'" v. 6 [October Memory Verse]

If I could have but one book of the Bible, it would be the Gospel of John. It presents Jesus as the One and only unique and eternal Son of God.

If I had to choose one chapter, it would be chapter 14. In it is the intimate conversation between Jesus and His disciples, just hours before His arrest. No literature compares to this in the entire world.

If I had only one verse in the entire Bible, it would be verse six. It encapsulates all that Jesus is to His followers. This verse alone is sufficient to bring us all the way to heavenly Glory. I urge you to embed it into your heart. It will keep you from the false philosophies and teachings of this world. It will show you the great "I AM" of the Bible.

See also: Ex. 3:13-14, 1 Tim. 2:5, 1 Jn. 4:9, 1 Jn. 5:20

October 19
Read John 14:7-11
"Whoever has seen Me has seen the Father" v. 9

    To define something means that it must be limited to our comprehension. We cannot define God. We can only describe Him, and so limited we are in doing that.
    I recently looked up the definition of God in the dictionary. God (capital 'G') was defined as, "The Supreme-Deity and self-existent Creator and upholder of the universe." A second definition said god (small 'g') is "A person or thing being honored or admired… One of various beings conceived of as being supernatural." Throughout history, man has had a propensity to create his own small 'g' god rather than look to the God who created him. This is still true today.
    Which God/god is yours — the original God or the new revised god?
    Jesus was very adamant that the only way to see the true God is by looking at Him. Any god absent of the Lord Jesus Christ is a false god.

See also: Eph. 1:3, 1 Jn. 5:20-21

October 20
Read John 14:10-14
"Greater works than these will he do" v. 12

    A man who was a notorious drinker for years was gloriously converted to the Lord Jesus Christ. The change was so real that no one could deny it. One day he met an old drinking buddy who asked him, "Now that you are a Christian, can you change water into wine for us?" The new Christian said, "No, I can't. But the wine I drank is now milk for my children!"
    Which is the greater miracle: The changing of water into wine, or the changing of a man's heart so he now buys milk and bread for his family rather than alcohol? Proof of our salvation always comes out in our actions. A change of heart always results in a changed life. Changing wine into milk —what a miracle!

See also: 1 Cor. 6:9-11, 2 Cor. 5:17, Gal. 6:15

October 21
Read John 14:12-14

"Whatever you ask in My name, this I will do, that the Father may be glorified in the Son" v. 13

Prayer can do anything that God can do. Prayer taps into Omnipotence.

Jesus' promise of answered prayer is (v. 12) in the contest of doing great exploits for God. Much of the "greater works" that we do is done through prayer. Prayer is the most powerful thing we can do. Jesus' promise of our potential of prayer in John 14:13 goes as follows:

Whatever	The Scope of prayer
Ask	The Condition of prayer
In My name	The Grounds of prayer
I will do	The Certainty of prayer
That the Father may be glorified in the Son	The Purpose of prayer

This should give us new confidence to pray with boldness!

See also: Rom. 8:26-27, Eph. 6:18, Js. 5:16-18

October 22
Read John 14:15-17

"And I will ask the Father, and He will give you another Helper, to be with you forever, even the Spirit of truth" v. 16-17

Jesus often called the Holy Spirit the Spirit of truth (John 15:26, 16:13). Every translation I have looked has a capital 'S' on Spirit. But for the sake of discussion, let's put a small 's' on it. Do you have a spirit of truth?

Are you a truthful person? Or are you deceptive? Do you twist facts to fit your argument? Or do people know you to be an honest person, a person of integrity? Have you determined to be truthful in every aspect of your life? Is honesty a hallmark of your character?

A spirit of falsehood cannot properly communicate truth. See Acts 16:16-18 for an example. If truth comes from a deceptive spirit it will naturally be questioned. If a person does not have a spirit of truth, are you sure that he has the Spirit of truth?

See also: Eph. 4:25, Eph. 5:15, 1 Tim. 4:1, Js. 5:12, 1 Jn. 4:6

October 23
Read John 14:18-21

"Whoever has My commandments and keeps them, he it is who loves Me. And He who loves Me will be loved by My Father, and I will love him and manifest Myself to him" v. 21

Love of course begins with God. But His love needs to be received and returned. Imagine what it would be like if a man loved a woman but she was indifferent. His love wouldn't be complete. God loves you. But His love isn't made perfect until you respond. When you do, love flows from Heaven to you and back to Heaven, continuing the cycle over and over. True love is not static. It is continuously flowing. Keep your love cycle always flowing and growing with God. The hymn writer, Charles Wesley put it this way:

> Love divine, all loves excelling, Joy of Heaven to earth come down;
> Fix in us Thy humble dwelling; All thy faithful mercies crown.
> Jesus, Thou art all compassion, Pure unbounded love Thou art;
> Visit us with Thy salvation; Enter every trembling heart.

See also: 2 Cor. 5:14-15, 1 Jn. 5:3, Rev. 2:4

October 24
Read John 14:18-25

"If anyone loves Me, he will keep My word, and My Father will love him, and we will come to him and make our home with him" v. 23

A machinist can tool a $5.00 piece of metal and make it worth $500.00 —That's skill.

An artist can take a canvas, paint a picture on it and make it worth $1000 — That's art.

Longfellow could take a sheet of paper, write a poem on it and make it worth $6000 —That's genius.

Rockefeller could sign his name to a piece of paper and make it worth a million dollars — That's capital.

But God can take a sinful soul, put His Spirit into it and fit it for Heaven —That's salvation! (Copied)

See also: Ezek. 36:26, 2 Cor. 6:17-18, Eph. 5:18

October 25
Read John 14:25-31

"Peace I leave with you; My peace I give to you. Not as the world gives do I give to you" v. 27

When you leave this world, there are only two things that matter: 1. Your destiny, (where you go) and 2. Your legacy, (what you leave behind). Jesus left a legacy for His disciples—His peace.

When we become Christians we have peace with God (Romans 5:1). But as we live in this world we can have the peace of God as well (Philippians 4:7). This personal peace is not something we manufacture from ourselves but something imparted from above. It is Christ's legacy to each of His children no matter what their circumstances.

See also: Is. 9:6-7, Is. 26:3, Phil. 4:7, Phil. 4:9, Col. 3:15

October 26
Read Mark 14:22-26

"And when they had sung a hymn, they went out to the Mount of Olives" v. 26

Jesus' last formal act with His disciples was to lead them in singing a hymn. Oh, how I wish I could have been there! Scottish politician Andrew Fletcher said, "Let me write the songs for a nation, and I care not who writes its laws". He was trying to illustrate the power that music has over the minds and hearts of people. Even being filled with the Holy Spirit is connected with singing (Ephesians 5:18-20). One of the chief activities of Heaven will be singing. What a joy it will be to join our voices in the heavenly anthems! I can't wait!

Missionaries never considered the church to be established in a nation until they were writing their own songs. Likewise, the writing of new songs by each generation promises that the church will continue. How important music is!

Psalm 40:3 says, "He put a new song in my mouth, a song of praise to God". The remainder of the verse tells what the result of that song will be —"Many will fear and put their trust in the Lord." Ask the Lord to put a new song in your heart today!

See also: Ps. 40:3, Ps. 100:1-5, Ps. 149:1-9, Acts 16:25

October 27
Read John 15:1-4

"Already you are clean because of the word that I have spoken to you" v. 3

When one is being interviewed for ordination as a pastor, a question usually asked is "How is your thought life?" What do you think about when your mind is free? That question gets to the very heart of who we are.

Our lives are lived in the realm of our minds—our thoughts. As we think, so we are. Everything we do begins first with a thought. Right actions are the result of right thoughts. Wrong actions are the result of wrong thoughts.

"Sow a thought, reap an action. Sow an action, reap a habit. Sow a habit, reap a character. Sow a character, reap a life. Sow a life, reap a destiny" (Copied). It all begins with those little things called thoughts.

In this world, there are certainly many wrong thoughts and attitudes. How do we keep our minds from being contaminated by them? Hearing God's word cleanses our minds. This enables us to think the very thoughts of Christ. The Bible calls this having a renewed or transformed mind.

See also: Rom. 8:5, Rom. 12:2, Col. 3:2

October 28
Read John 15:1-8

"Abide in Me, and I in you …the branch cannot bear fruit by itself, unless it abides in the vine " v. 4

If you or I went to a professional baseball game and stepped up to the plate to bat, no doubt our career would end with three pitches. But imagine if the home run hero of the team could get inside of us. One swing of the bat would earn us the admiration of everyone in the stadium! It would be his strength, his ability, his skill inside us that gets results.

The sooner we realize that we are incapable of living the Christian life, the better off we are. We need the power of another—even Jesus who lives inside of us by His Spirit—in order to be fruitful as Christians. And that power is available. Abide in Him.

See also: 1 Jn. 2:14, 1 Jn. 2:27-28, 1 Jn. 3:6

October 29
Read John 15:1-8

"I am the vine; you are the branches. Whoever abides in Me and I in him, he it is that bears much fruit, for apart from Me you can do nothing" v. 5

Have you come to the strong realization that without Christ you can do nothing acceptable to God? There is nothing in our old nature that He can accept. Everything that emanates from the Adam nature is tainted. And the perishable cannot inherit the imperishable. (1 Cor. 15:50).

But the opposite is also true. Phil. 4:13 says, "I can do all things through Him who strengthens me". I never read John 15:5 without also thinking of Phil. 4:13. If you write in your Bible, put that verse in the margin beside John 15:5.

See also: Rom. 7:18, 2 Cor. 12:9, Eph. 3:16

October 30
Read John 15:7-11

"If you abide in Me and My words abide in you, ask whatever you wish, and it will be done for you" v. 7

Who is the most influential person in your church? Is it the person with the big name in the community? Or is it the one with the most money? Or is it the one who is the most vocal when church decisions are being discussed?

Does a person need to hold an office of authority to be influential? According to the Bible, the person who can effectively pray is the most influential. He has an audience not with man but with God. His appeals go all the way to the throne of God.

If you want to have a position of authority in the Kingdom of God, don't seek it from man, but from God through prayer.

See also: Ps. 6:9, Js. 5:16-18

October 31
Read John 15:15-17

"You did not choose Me, but I chose you and appointed you that you should go forth and bear fruit and that your fruit should abide" v. 16

Remember in school when teams were chosen to play games? Imagine being the last one chosen. I always felt sorry for that person. His team didn't want him. They said they would be better off without him. Though he wanted so much to play and contribute to his team, he knew he was unwanted. He was a liability and not an asset. How humiliating!

John 15:16 tells us we are on a different team — a team with Jesus Christ as the captain! He saw something of value in you and personally chose you to be on His team! You are important! You have a special role to play to bring His team to victory.

With God's appointing also comes His anointing. Knowing that you are of great value to the Team Captain, go forth today and bear fruit. Remember also that we are playing on a team that cannot lose!

See also: Eph. 1:4, Col. 1:10, 1 Pet. 2:9-11

November 1
Read John 15:17-21

"If the world hates you, know that it has hated Me before it hated you" v. 18

The Christian has three mortal enemies he will battle against throughout his life: 1. The devil — The same evil being that Adam encountered in the Garden of Eden. 2. The flesh — Your Adam nature / your own heart, which is in rebellion against God. 3. The world — The system of fallen man which is alienated from God. Don't be surprised when you are attacked and tempted by any of these three entities.

The Bible tells us two things about the world system: First, it will hate you (Yes, hate you). We are lights that expose their evil deeds. Second, don't love it. It will pull you away from God.

The battle is on. The stakes are high. Hard struggles are ahead. But you have One who never lost a battle at your side!

See also: Rom. 12:2, Eph. 6:12, Js. 4:4, 1 Jn. 2:15-17, 1 Jn. 3:13, 1 Jn. 4:4

November 2
Read John 15:18-21

"If they persecuted Me, they will also persecute you" v. 20

In days long ago, a treasure seeker had a fool-proof way of testing the gems he obtained. He would put the gem on a hard surface and stomp on it with the heel of his boot. If it shattered, it was worthless. If it got only a scratch, it was of some value. But if the blow of his heel left no scratch, he knew he had a gem of rare value. Sometimes the treasure-seeker would deliver blow after blow on the rare stone just to prove its worth.

In a very real sense, the world has the right to know if we are genuine or not. Their method of finding out is often as crude as the treasure-seeker's boot of by-gone days.

How will you fare when the boot of persecution delivers its blow on your soul? If you endure, even the people of the world will recognize the value of your faith.

See also: Job 23:10, Js. 1:2-4, 1 Pet. 1:6-7

November 3
Read John 15:26-16:4

"The Spirit of truth, who proceeds from the Father, He will bear witness about Me" v. 26

The word "trinity" is never found in the Bible. But many verses such as John 15:26 make reference to the triune Godhead.

Many people today often say that they have the spirit. But I sometimes wonder what spirit they have. It doesn't always seem that it is the Holy Spirit. 1 John 4:1 says, "Do not believe every spirit, but test the spirits to see whether they are from God." How can you be sure that it is the Holy Spirit?

Jesus said the Holy Spirit—the Spirit of Truth—will point people to Him. Any spirit that does not point you to Jesus and His cross is a false spirit. Beware: there are many spirits that are not of God.

The next time you go to church and a sermon is given, ask yourself, "Where is Jesus? Where is the cross?" If you don't see Jesus or His cross, are you sure the Spirit of Truth is there?

See also: 1 Cor. 2:2, 1 Jn. 4:3

November 4
Read John 16:1-7

"It is to your advantage that I go away, for if I do not go away, the Helper will not come to you. But if I go, I will send Him to you" v. 7

When my son was about ten years old, we got on our bicycles and set out for the tennis court. To get there, we had to cross a state highway — a real challenge for a father and son on bicycles. As we crossed the busy intersection, my instructions to Matthew were, "Stay right beside me and listen to what I say". With cars and trucks racing by I wanted him to do one thing — listen to my voice. With the temptations to stop or turn, his instructions were to stay beside me. He did just fine, and we had a very memorable time both getting to the tennis court and playing.

Jesus said that the Holy Spirit would be our counselor and helper. The word in Greek means 'one who comes beside'. As my son was to me on our bicycle adventure, so are we to be to the Holy Spirit. As we listen to Him and stay beside Him, He will direct us through the dangerous intersections of life.

See also: Ps. 16:8, Ps. 23:4, Is. 30:21, Is. 43:2, 2 Cor. 6:16

November 5
Read John 16:7-11

"When He comes, He will convict the world concerning sin and righteousness and judgment" v. 8

Prevenient grace is the working of the Holy Spirit in the circumstances and heart of a person before he comes to Christ. The Spirit's purpose is to bring a person to see his sin and turn from it. If you are saved, you can look back at your BC life and see where God worked through circumstances long before you gave your life to Him. That is prevenient grace.

Joel 2:28 tells us that in the last days God will pour out His Spirit on all flesh. For the believer, it is the Spirit of power. For the unbeliever, it is the Spirit of conviction working His prevenient grace. He is doing this in the lives of your unsaved friend right now. As you speak of Christ to him, you can be certain that the Holy Spirit has already been working in that life for years to bring him to conviction and repentance. Pray that God will bring His work of prevenient grace to completion in that life. Then, get ready. Your friend will soon come to Jesus!

See also: Acts 11:18, Acts 17:30, Rom. 2:4, 2 Cor. 7:10

November 6
Read John 16:12-15

"He will glorify Me, for He will take what is mine and declare it to you" v. 14

If you wish to know about the working of the Holy Spirit in our lives, get acquainted with John chapters 14, 15, and 16. These are the words of Jesus Himself. The Holy Spirit always points to Jesus and His cross. Please note that any spirit not pointing to Jesus is not the Spirit of God. This is the spirit of antichrist. As we approach the end of the age, this deceptive spirit will become more prevalent. The primary way it is manifested today is in the spirit of self-improvement, or self-worth, or self-fulfillment. Note that 'self' replaces Christ. Self is glorified rather than Christ. You will hear this deceptive doctrine taught in many contemporary churches today. Be warned!

See also: 2 Thess. 2:9-12, 1 Jn. 2:22, 1 Jn. 4:3, 2 Jn. 1:7

November 7
Read John 16:16-24

"You will be sorrowful, but your sorrow will turn into joy" v. 20

The Gospel makes people first mad, then sad, and last, glad. It makes us <u>mad</u> when we are told that our self-righteousness is not sufficient when standing before a holy God (Isaiah 64:6). Then it makes us <u>sad</u> when we realize that Christ agonized on the cross in our place (1 Peter 3:18). After the sadness of repentance, our hearts get <u>glad</u> to see the risen Christ who took our sins away (John 20:20).

1 Timothy 1:15 says, "The saying is trustworthy and deserving of full acceptance, that Christ Jesus came into the world to save sinners, of whom I am the foremost". He came to save sinners. Sinners like me. Sinners like you. How does that make you feel: mad, sad or glad?

See also: Jer. 17:9, Acts 2:37, Rom. 5:2

November 8
Read John 16:25-33

"I came from the Father and have come into the world, and now I am leaving the world and going to the Father" v. 28

A vagabond is someone who has no home. A stranger is someone away from home. A fugitive is someone running from home. A foreigner is someone in another person's home. A pilgrim is someone on his way home.

The Bible classifies believers as strangers in the world (Hebrews 11:13-16). We are citizens of another country. This world is not our home. We are looking for a city whose Designer and Builder is God (Hebrews 11:10). What a joy it will be to finally get there! Let's not get too comfortable here!

See also: Ps. 84:5, Phil. 3:20, 1 Pet. 1:1, 1 Pet. 2:11

November 9
Read John 17:1-5

'I glorified You on earth, having accomplished the work You gave Me to do" v. 4

Jesus, knowing that the Jewish officials were at that moment plotting His crucifixion, and within only a few hours He would be on the cross, alone, bleeding, dying, forsaken by all, was not hurried or worried. He did not pray, "O God, I have failed". He, with peace in His heart, simply looked up into the face of His Father and said, "I have glorified You". And to glorify God is the ultimate purpose of life.

The dictionary defines success as, 'the gaining of wealth, respect or fame'. Jesus defined success as doing the will of God. "I have glorified You on earth, having accomplished the work You gave me to do". What joy if on the day of our death, similar words can be spoken by us!

See also: Phil. 1:21-25, 2 Tim. 4:6-8

November 10
Read John 17:6-16

"I do not ask that You take them out of the world, but that You keep them from the evil one" v. 15

    A Christian in the world is like a ship in the ocean. A ship in the ocean is great. But the ocean in a ship is disaster! The Bible makes it clear that we are in this world system, but we are not to be a part of it. Our true citizenship is not of this world.

    At times we are like the Israelites who crossed the Red Sea but their hearts were still back in Egypt. It took God only a little while to get them out of Egypt. But it took Him forty years to get Egypt out of them.

    If we allow the world into our hearts, we will eventually sink spiritually. Let's fortify ourselves against such a temptation.

See also: Js. 4:4, 1 Jn. 2:15-17

November 11
Read John 17:12-19

"For their sake I consecrate myself" v. 19

    Is it okay to have alcohol in my refrigerator? Or go fishing on Sunday instead of going to church? Or participate in a host of other activities that others think is wrong? One biblical principle to follow in such cases is that if it causes other people to stumble, we shouldn't do it. Our motivation is not legalism but love.

    As we live in this world, <u>license</u> permits us to do about anything we desire. On the other end of the spectrum is <u>legalism</u>, which is very restricting. Both extremes are wrong. Between the two is the law of <u>liberty</u> and love. We should consecrate (separate) ourselves from certain things not necessarily because they are inherently wrong, but for the sake of others who may be weaker in the faith. Let us govern our lives by this principle.

See also: Rom. 14:13-23, 1 Cor. 8:7-13, Gal. 5:1

November 12
Read John 17:20-26

"That they may all be one just as You, Father, are in Me, and I in You, that they also may be in Us" v. 21

My wife and I went to a volleyball game. The very first period I noticed two girls from the visiting team arguing with one another as they were on the court. I leaned over and pointed it out to my wife and confidently predicted that they were going to lose. Sure enough — they lost!

Were you ever in a church where different factions had disputes? Rather than uniting their forces and working for the cause of Christ, they waste their energy fighting one another. Another sick, ineffective church. How sad. And then we wonder why people of the world don't come.

Let us pray Jesus' prayer of John 17:21 over our church.

See also: Gal. 5:15, Phil. 2:3, Phil 4:2

November 13
Read Matthew 26:36-46

"Then Jesus went with them to a place called Gethsemane" v. 36

If you set your soul to follow Jesus, sooner or later your path will lead to Gethsemane. It is a place of great anguish of soul. It is a place that no one else really knows about except you and God. Your friends, like Jesus' disciples, may be so indifferent to your plight that they will even sleep through it. But don't think it strange, for Jesus Himself endured it. Its final end is death to self and total surrender to the will of God.

You must go through your Gethsemane. But it is only a temporary stop. From that time on you will be a different person. From there you will go on to find the fullness of what God has for your life.
PS. You may need to go through Gethsemane more than once to relearn the necessity of dying to self.

See also: Phil. 2:5-8, Phil. 3:7-8

November 14
Read Luke 22:39-46

"Father, if you are willing, remove this cup from Me. Nevertheless, not My will, but Yours be done" v. 42

It should always be a greater concern for us to be obedient than to be happy. It is more important to please God than to please ourselves. If we make it our goal to please God, we put ourselves in the place of His favor, even if it means temporary suffering.

The will of God is always best even if it means taking our cross and bearing it for His sake. Therefore, rather than trying to get God to do our will, let us purpose to do His will no matter what the cost. Please remember also that the will of God will never lead you where the grace of God cannot keep you.

See also: Rom. 8:18, Eph. 6:6-7, 1 Pet. 5:10

November 15
Read Luke 22:39-46

"And there appeared to Him an angel from Heaven, strengthening Him" v. 43

There were angels at Jesus' birth. Again, they were at His temptation. In Gethsemane an angel strengthened Him. We also see angelic activity when He arose and again when He ascended to Heaven. But there were no angels at His crucifixion. There were twelve legions of angels standing ready to attack (Matthew 26:53), but they were never given the word to do so. At His crucifixion, He was alone — all alone, forsaken not only by His friends but also by the heavenly powers. He took our sin alone. He bore the wrath of God alone. He took the punishment of your sin and my sin all alone. He did all this so we could be with Him forever. What a wonderful Savior! Thank You, Lord.

See also: Is. 53:4-6, 1 Pet. 2:24

November 16
Read Matthew 26:47-56

"Do you think that I cannot appeal to My Father, and He will at once send Me more than twelve legions of angels?" v. 53

Of all my experiences in the Air Force, my greatest story is the night I met the Supreme Commander of the universe. He had scars in His hands and feet, but otherwise, He was in GREAT shape! (Read Revelation 1:13-15 for His description) Our Great Commander has legions of mighty warriors on His side that no Roman army could resist. Neither can the modern militaries of our day withstand them.

I have never met a man bigger than Jesus. He conquered sin. He conquered Satan. He conquered death. He has also conquered the hearts of everyone who has met Him. He has never lost a battle. And I am convinced that He will not lose the war. Though strife goes on around you, trust Him. Trust Him!

See also: Josh. 5:13-15, Rev. 1:13-18

November 17
Read John 18:1-9

"When Jesus said to them, 'I am He', they drew back and fell to the ground" v. 6

Some hymns should never be forgotten. Here is a verse from one of them:

> Holy, Holy, Holy! All the saints adore Thee,
>
> Casting down their golden crowns around the glassy sea:
>
> Cherubim and seraphim falling down before Thee,
>
> Which wert and art, and ever-more shall be.

When God appeared to one of His people in days of old, they fell forward on their faces. When He revealed Himself to His enemies, they fell backward.

Those big strong soldiers could not endure three little words of Jesus — "I am He". No wonder, for Jesus was referring to Himself being the incarnation of the Great 'I Am' in Exodus 3:13-15. Just imagine the utter dread of those who rejected Him on the day of His return. But what inexpressible joy to those who are looking for Him!

See also: Josh. 5:14, Acts 9:3-5, Rev. 1:17-18, Rev. 6:16

November 18
Read Luke 22:47-53

"Jesus said, 'No more of this!' And He touched his ear and healed him" v. 51

If we attempt to accomplish God's will by carnal methods, we accomplish no more than Peter did when he cut off Malchus' ear (John 18:10). We only get in God's way and create problems that He then needs to heal. God does not need our carnal efforts. He wants our obedience.

We should continuously remember that the weapons of our warfare are not carnal but spiritual. We need to learn, as Peter did, that our fight is not with swords and spears, but with love and truth. If we do that, He is more than able to take care of Himself without our assistance. And He will take care of us at the same time!

See also: 2 Cor. 10:4, Eph. 6:10-12

November 19
Read Matthew 26:57-68

"Jesus said to him, 'You have said so. But I tell you, from now on you will see the Son of Man seated at the right hand of Power and coming on the clouds of Heaven'" v. 64

Jesus, the Son of God (v. 63), came to earth to represent God. Then as the Son of Man (v. 64), He went to Heaven to represent man. Jesus called Himself the Son of Man in reference to Daniel 7:13-14. He was claiming to be the One who would come before the Ancient of Days on man's behalf. This made the high priest furious. But it was the High Priest of the ages that stood before him.

Once it was recognized who He was, it was time for Him to go to the cross and become our sacrifice. It is amazing how the misguided efforts of the High Priest fulfilled the plan of God.

See also: Lev. 24:16, Acts 7:56, Heb. 4:14, Rev. 1:13

November 20
Read Matthew 26:69-75

"Then (Peter) began to invoke a curse on himself and to swear, 'I do not know the man'" v. 74

At first glance we may think that Judas' betrayal and Peter's denial are the same thing, but they are very different. One was done out of wickedness while the other was done out of weakness.

Many times when we in weakness do something contrary to our values, we then allow ourselves to be beaten down, and live in a state of defeat. God never intended this.

In Numbers 20 where Moses struck the rock rather than speaking to it as God commanded, he was told he would not enter the Promised Land. But Moses did not sit down and lament. He got up and continued doing the will of God until his life was finished.

We have all done things that we regret. But God does not want us to sit in a state of defeat. He wants us to get up and serve Him anew. He will restore you just as He restored Peter.

See also: Num. 20:10-13, 1 Tim. 1:13-14

November 21
Read Matthew 27:11-23

"Now Jesus stood before the governor, and the governor asked Him, 'Are You the King of the Jews?'" v. 11

In Pilate's query of Jesus, he asked three questions. Paraphrased, his questions were: 1. " Who are You?"(v. 11) 2. "What have You done?" (v. 23) and, 3. "What should I do with Jesus?" (v. 22)

I would contend that these are the three most important questions in the world. The early church diligently hammered out the answer to these questions in its creeds. Thankfully they got the right answers. Every generation since has found the need to again ask these same questions and answer them for themselves.

Pilate asked the right questions. Sadly, he did not wait for the right answers. Now these questions are placed before you. Who is Jesus? What has He done? What will you do with Him? Maybe you can give a quick answer. But to ponder them will take a lifetime.

See also: Phil. 2:6-11, Col. 1:15-20, Heb. 1:2-4

November 22
Read John 18:33-37

"My kingdom is not of this world. If My kingdom were of this world, my servants would have been fighting" v. 36

When Constantine heard of Christ's crucifixion, he said, "If I had been there, that righteous man would not have died". He would have (he thought) driven off the executioners with sword and spear. The crusaders came in the same spirit when they held swords to the necks of peasants saying , "Accept Christ or die." Clearly in their zeal they did not have the Spirit of Christ.

Often the worst enemies of the cause of Christ are people within the church who try to get a spiritual end by carnal means. It doesn't work. We do not make converts to Christ by arguing and threatening. Christ's Kingdom is not of this world. Therefore our weapons and tactics are not of this world. God's purpose is not that we defeat our enemies but that we win them. Let us not go with the love of power but the power of love as we seek to advance the Kingdom of God.

See also: Ps. 2:1-12, 2 Cor. 10:3-4

November 23
Read Matthew 27:20-26

"Pilate said to them, 'Then what shall I do with Jesus who is called Christ?'" v. 22

On the fateful day of Jesus' arrest, we find that it was Pilate and not Jesus who was actually on trial. It was his destiny and not Jesus' that was at stake.

There comes a time in everyone's life when a person comes face to face with the Living Christ, and a decision must be made. No matter what the decision is, from that point on that person is never the same again. Pilate made his decision in favor of the yelling mob and the acclaim of Caesar. Tradition tells us that three years later, he committed suicide.

"What shall I do with Jesus?" That is the most important question anyone will ever answer. No one else can answer it for you. You cannot evade Him. You cannot remain neutral. You cannot wash your hands of the matter. A decision must be made. What will you do with Jesus?

See also: Josh. 24:15, 1 Kings 18:21, Acts 13:46, 2 Cor. 5:20

November 24
Read Luke 23:18-25

"But they were urgent, demanding with loud cries that He should be crucified. And their voices prevailed" v. 23

The same city that heard 'Hosanna in the highest' at Jesus' triumphal entry, heard 'Crucify Him' just five days later. Their voices prevailed over truth and righteousness and honesty. How fickle man is!

There is no room for passive indifference when it comes to Christ. We either bow and call Him Lord or we shout "Away with this man." There was no casual observer on that day in Jerusalem, and neither will there be when He returns.

Imagine when the armies of this world gather in the Valley of Jezreel to fight against one another, and they train their weapons on the King of kings as He returns in the sky! (Revelation 19:11-21) But their efforts will be as futile as their first century counterparts who nailed Him to the cross. And then again, the cry of 'Hosanna' will go up from the streets of Jerusalem and around the world as His own welcome Him as their King!

See also: Rev. 16:16, Rev. 19:6

November 25
Read John 19:1-11

"You would have no authority over Me at all unless it had been given you from above" v. 11

I recently heard a man on television news stating that there is a conspiracy to subvert and destroy our nation. Is this true or isn't it? We rightly should be concerned for our nation and work in every legitimate way to preserve and protect our liberties. But we need to realize the greater truth that God is in control. World and international affairs are not in man's hands but God's. He still reigns. His throne is secure.

Our founders stated in the Declaration of Independence that in their efforts they had "a firm reliance on the protection of Divine Providence." Is not that Providence still working today in the affairs of men? Revelation 1:5 refers to Jesus as "The ruler of kings on earth". Therefore don't fear. Look to His providence. If your god can't help you, get a bigger God!

See also: Ps. 46:1-11, Rom. 8:28

November 26
Read Mark 15:6-15

"So Pilate, wishing to satisfy the crowd, released for them Barabbas, and having scourged Jesus, he delivered Him to be crucified" v. 15

I am told of a painting of the crucifixion of Jesus by the famous Dutch artist Rembrandt. The cross and the Christ are in the center of the picture. Around the cross are the women, the soldiers and others. Off to the side of the picture in the shadows is Rembrandt himself! He wanted to show that he was also responsible for Christ's crucifixion.

The apostle Paul asserted that he was also responsible for Christ's death (1 Timothy 1:15). And so was I. And so were you. And so was every person on this earth who has ever drawn a breath. Each of us is personally responsible. But the good news is that when we acknowledge our egregious part we find forgiveness and grace.

See also: Rom. 3:23-24, Rom. 5:10, Col. 1:21-22, 1 Jn. 2:2

November 27
Read Luke 23:33-38

"And when they came to the place that is called The Skull, there they crucified Him" v. 33

It was the experience of a lifetime, my trip to Israel. Words can't express the final day as we walked through the Mount of Olives, viewed the Eastern Gate, toured the temple area, and walked the Via Dolorosa. We wanted to linger at each site. But our guide kept urging us to keep moving.

As the sun was setting, we got to the base of Mount Calvary. It was then that I realized why our guide kept prompting us to hurry. His words: "I'm sorry, but the gate to Mount Calvary is closed for the night. We won't be able to enter." As the night darkened, I sadly turned back, never to walk on that holy site.

I saw so many beautiful places in Israel. But I never got to Mount Calvary. In spite of all the wonderful experiences, I never got to the place where my Savior died for me.

You may attend church. You may enjoy the fellowship, be encouraged by the singing, appreciate the preaching. But have you been to Calvary? If not, let me be your guide and ask you not to linger. The gate of God's mercy is still open. But the night is coming. I urge you to get to Calvary before it is forever too late.

See also: Rom. 13:11, 1 Thess. 5:6, 1 Pet. 4:7

November 28
Read John 19:17-22

"And He went out, bearing His own cross, to the place called The Place of the Skull, which in Aramaic is called Golgotha" v. 17

The universal symbol of the Christian faith is the cross. As the earth circles the Sun, so our faith revolves around the cross of Jesus. The cross is:

<u>High</u> enough to reach to the highest Heaven, the very throne of God

<u>Long</u> enough to reach through all the millennia from the beginning of time until the end

<u>Deep</u> enough to reach to the lowest, most vile of sinners, to the gates of hell itself

<u>Wide</u> enough to reach to every person of every culture or language around the world   (Copied)

See also: Is. 53:4-6, Gal. 6:14

November 29
Read John 19:17-22

"He went out, bearing His own cross, to the place called The Place of the Skull…There they crucified Him" v. 17-18

I remember seeing a picture of Jesus being crucified. Everything seemed so authentic — the crown of thorns; the drops of blood; the anguish on my Savior's face. But instead of Him being crucified on Golgotha, the artist depicted Him as being crucified in a metropolitan city. As businessmen walked by, a jet flew overhead, and cars waited at the light, Jesus hung there on the street corner dying.

Although we can challenge the historic and geographic aspect of the picture, the artist's spiritual message was clear — He died for us who are living today. An even more personal depiction of Christ's crucifixion would be to see Him dying just outside the door of our house.

Although we have advanced so far technologically, we still need a Savior. It is still necessary to look to His substitutionary sacrifice on our behalf. He died for you personally. Have you personally appropriated His finished work?

See also: 1 Pet. 3:18, 1 Jn. 2:2

November 30
Read Matthew 27:33-38

"Then two robbers were crucified with Him, one on the right and one on the left" v. 38

If you took a drive across the Rocky Mountains, eventually you would come to a sign that says, 'Continental Divide'. At that point, if two drops of rain fell only inches apart, one drop would make its way to the Gulf of Mexico, while the other would eventually end up in the Pacific Ocean.

As there is a continental divide, so there also is a spiritual divide. We are either on Christ's right or His left. He will either be silent to our plight or we will hear the words, "Today you shall be with Me in paradise". Only Christ can occupy the center cross. Our view of His cross will determine our destiny. On which side of His cross are you?

See also: Deut. 30:19, 1 Jn. 5:11-12

December 1
Read Luke 23:33-38

"Father, forgive them, for they know not what they do" v. 34

When Jesus was nailed to the cross, His first words were not accusations or threats or pronouncements of judgment, but words of forgiveness. Isn't it amazing how many times He does things just the opposite of what you or I would do? His first statement from the cross was a plea for the very ones who whipped Him, spit on Him and pounded the nails through His hands. What grace! He knew vividly that the person with the real dilemma was not the victim but the perpetrator.

Is there something in your past that you regret? Is there a dark memory you wish you could forget? If Jesus could forgive His executioners, He can forgive you! I believe if you could go to the cross and see Jesus hanging there, He would lift up His eyes, look at you, speak your name and say "I forgive you".

Someone has said that the best communication is from the heart, to the heart. Receive into your heart the words from His heart — "I forgive you".

See also: Ps. 32:5, Acts 2:38-39, Acts 13:38, 1 Jn. 1:9

December 2
Read Matthew 27:38-43

"If You are the Son of God, come down from the cross" v. 40

When George Washington was a teen, his older brother Lawrence had a debilitating illness. The doctors thought if he went to a warmer climate it would help him. He went to Barbados, an island in the Caribbean, with little brother George to assist him. Sadly, Lawrence died. George contracted smallpox while there. What good came out of such a trip?

In the winter of 1777, at Valley Forge, a smallpox epidemic broke out. But because General Washington had the disease years earlier, he was immune. The epidemic had no effect on him. While some may call it coincidence, I prefer to call it providence.

"If you are the Son of God..." That is the same challenge Satan gave Jesus in the wilderness at the beginning of His ministry (Matthew. 4:3 and 6). Victory over temptation in the wilderness paved the way for His victory over temptation on the cross.

I think God works in a similar way today, allowing us to go through tests, knowing that we will face greater tests down the road. By His providence, He even uses the bad times to strengthen us for what is ahead. Let's be certain that we pass the first test in private so we can also pass the second test in public.

See also: Gen. 50:20, 1 Sam. 17:34-37, Jer. 29:11, Rom. 8:28

December 3
Read Mark 15:21-32

"Let the Christ, the King of Israel, come down now from the cross that we may see and believe" v. 32

Jesus' mockers in the above verse made two errors. First, they said they wanted Him to come down from the cross. But it was God's plan that He come up from the grave — a far greater miracle! Christ's great power is revealed not in evading death, but in conquering it! If Jesus had done what they suggested, death would still have dominion over us.

The second mistake they made was that they said they wanted to see and believe. God's order is that we would first believe and then see. Seeing a miracle does not automatically produce faith.

How thankful we should be that Jesus did not show His power by evading death, but by conquering it. If you believe this, you will then see that it is true.

See also: 1 Cor. 15:20, 1 Pet. 1:8-9

December 4
Read Luke 23:33-43

"If You are the King of the Jews, save Yourself" v. 37

God never leaves Himself without a witness. He even used Balaam's donkey as His spokesman! (Numbers 22:28-30) But who witnessed to the thief on the cross? The disciples were in hiding. Jesus' followers were silenced. That was when His accusers mocked Him about being the King. As they did, the thief, in spite of their mocking tone, recognized who Jesus was and responded to Him in faith!

If believers will not bring praise to God, He can even raise up scoffers to do it! If someone is scoffing at you because of your faith, perhaps it is not because you have said too much about your Savior, but you haven't said enough. Speak up for Him. His word will not return void.

See also: Ps. 76:10, Is. 55:10-11, Rom. 1:19-20

December 5
Read Matthew 27:39-44

" He is the King of Israel; let Him come down now from the cross, and we will believe in Him" v. 42

Colonel George W. Goethals endured intense criticism as he engineered and dug the Panama Canal. One of his subordinates asked him if he was going to answer his critics. "I will in time," said Goethals, "with a canal!" On April 15, 1914, the canal opened, and every critic was silenced!

While on the cross, Jesus' accusers taunted Him and told Him to come down. But He answered not a word — until the following Sunday! He dispelled every criticism by rising from the dead!

Is Jesus who He claimed to be? Can He do what He promised? Absolutely! His resurrection proves it. Let us remember that as we endure criticism for the name of Christ.

See also: Gal. 6:9, Heb. 12:2

December 6
Read Luke 23:36-43

"One of the criminals who were hanged railed at Him ... But the other rebuked him ..." v. 39-40

We can see all of mankind represented in the two criminals at Jesus' right and left hand. The difference in points of view of the center cross determines our destiny. They can be compared as follows:

Three different crosses:	The rejecter's cross
	The Redeemer's cross
	The receiver's cross
Three different men:	A dying sinner
	A dying Savior
	A dying saint
Three different deaths:	One died in sin
	One died for sin
	One died unto sin

See also: 1 Cor. 1:23-24, 1 Cor. 2:2

December 7
Read Luke 23:39-43

"Jesus, remember me when You come into your kingdom" v. 42

One thief was saved that none needs to despair — but only one, that none should presume. Both of them asked to be saved, but only one was saved. One wished to be saved from his circumstances. The other wanted to be saved from his sin. One was concerned about his situation. The other was concerned about his soul. One was concerned about his skin, while the other was sorry for his sin.

The unrepentant thief wanted to live so he could go back and sin more, while the repentant thief was willing to die so he could live anew in the kingdom of Christ. Jesus never responded to the one prayer, while He answered the other with the absolute assurance of eternal life. Perhaps this is why some people's prayer for salvation is not answered, while others experience great joy and change.

These two men stand on opposite sides of the spiritual divide which separates all mankind. On which side are you?

See also: Acts 13:46, 2 Thess. 3:2

December 8
Read Matthew 27:45-50

"About the ninth hour Jesus cried out with a loud voice, saying, 'Eli, Eli, lema sabachthani?' that is, 'My God, My God, why have You forsaken Me?'" v. 46

The Jewish calendar was marked by many feast days and days of celebration. But only one day per year was set aside for fasting — the day of Atonement. That was the day a lamb was sacrificed for their sins which pointed to the sacrifice of Christ. On that day, out of respect for the offering made for their souls, no food was to be eaten.

When Christ offered Himself for our sins, He fulfilled the ritual of the Day of Atonement. What better way could we observe Good Friday than by humbling ourselves through fasting? Fasting from 9:00 AM until 3:00 PM, the hours that Jesus was on the cross, will cause us to have a greater appreciation for Christ's atoning sacrifice on our behalf. Is this too much for us to ask when we realize what He has done for us? Why not give it a try on the next Good Friday?

See also: Lev. 23:26-32, Ps. 22:1, 1 Jn. 2:2

December 9
Read Mark 15:33-39

"And at the ninth hour Jesus cried out with a loud voice, 'Eloi, Eloi, lema sabachthani?' which means, 'My God, My God, why have You forsaken Me?'" v. 34

The very first reference to the cross is in Genesis 3:15. Just after Adam and Eve had sinned, God proclaimed to Satan that his head would be crushed by the seed of the woman. The bruising of His heel is a reference to Jesus' sufferings on the cross.

In Psalm 22:1, some 1000 years before the coming of Christ, King David penned the very words which Jesus spoke from the cross. God looked down through history and heard the words of Jesus on the cross. Then He revealed those words to David a millennium before it happened.

Jesus' death was not an accident. He was not a victim. Nor was He a martyr. His death was in the providence of God before time began. Through His sufferings, He became the Savior of the world.

He was forsaken so we could be forgiven. Are you trusting Him?

See also: Heb. 9:26, Rev. 5:5-6, Rev. 13:8

December 10
Read Matthew 28:1-10

"Come, see the place where He lay. Then go quickly and tell His disciples that He has risen from the dead" v. 7-8

God's calls and commands to us are exceedingly simple. In this case, "Come and see ... Go and tell..." The day I realized the mighty work Christ did for me by dying for my sins, I had a strong inclination that I must somehow tell others. And that is what I have daily endeavored to do since that day.

As soon as we see the mighty working of God, it is our responsibility to go and tell others. That is the essence of His call upon our lives. As we go, Jesus Himself will meet us and minister to us just as He did to these women. All we need to do is take the next simple step of obedience.

See also: Is. 6:8, Rom. 1:14-15, 1 Jn. 1:3

December 11
Read Matthew 28:1-10

"They departed quickly from the tomb with fear and great joy, and ran to tell the disciples. And behold, Jesus met them and said, 'Greetings!'" v. 8-9

The women believed that Jesus had risen from the dead before they physically saw Him. Jesus never appeared to unbelievers. He didn't go to Pilate or Herod or the Sanhedrin, but to His little band of believing disciples. And who does Christ reveal Himself to today? Not to the scoffers and skeptics, but to those who are seeking Him.

The world in its blindness continues with all its thoughts wrapped up in this life. It never seems to be able to lift its eyes to Heaven and see the greater reality. But thank God that those of us who believe that He truly is risen see Him with the eyes of our soul.

See also: 1 Cor. 1:18, 2 Cor. 4:4

December 12
Read Luke 24:1-12

"Why do you seek the living among the dead? He is not here, but has risen" v. 5-6

The last chapter of each of the four Gospels (last two chapters of John) changed everything. A man's story ends when he is put in the grave. But Jesus' story triumphs over the grave and goes on and on even to volumes yet unwritten!

A great chess player came across a painting of a chess match in which all mankind was on one side of the board and the Grim Reaper (death) was on the other side. Because death was winning, he had a sinister sneer on his face. After looking at the picture a while, the chess player announced, "One move and I can checkmate death."

The resurrection of Jesus from the dead is the one move that checkmated death! Death will shortly be swallowed up never to be known again in all of God's universe! It is only a matter of time and all creation will know. Right here, right now, today, believers can stand in the resurrection victory of Jesus Christ!

See also: Is. 25:8, 1 Cor. 15:22-26, Rev. 1:18, Rev. 21:4

December 13
Read John 20:11-18

"Jesus said to her, 'Woman, why are you weeping? Whom are you seeking?'" v. 15

It is interesting that we find what we are looking for. If a man came into a strange town looking for a casino, he would find one. If the same man came into a town looking for a church, he would find the church and never notice that the casino existed. In Mary's case, she was looking for a dead prophet instead of a living Savior. She was looking for a bloody corpse, not a risen triumphant Lord. Consequently, she did not recognize Him when Jesus Himself appeared to her and spoke to her.

How many times do people expect Jesus to be someone so much less than who He really is? Let's not limit Him by expecting Him to fit into the little box of our small minds.

See also: Eph. 1:20-23, Eph. 3:20-21

December 14
Read Mark 16:9-13

"Now when He rose early on the first day of the week, He appeared first to Mary Magdalene" v. 9

Why do Christians have their worship service on Sunday — particularly Sunday morning? Because that is the time that Jesus rose from the dead. That's good enough for me.

God told the Jews to worship Him on Saturday (the Sabbath) because that was the day He finished His work of creation, and entered into His rest (Exodus 20:8-11). Our seven day week is based on that concept. Some insist even today that we should worship on Saturday. But to do so would obligate us to adhere to every ceremonial law of the Old Testament — an impossible task.

On Sunday, the first day of the week, Jesus rose from the dead, beginning a new creation — the creation of those who are alive from the dead! Therefore, every Sunday, when I awake, as one of those who are raised with Christ, I get up and go to worship my Risen Lord.

See also: 2 Cor. 5:17, Eph. 2:5-6

December 15
Read Luke 24:36-43

"And when He had said this, He showed them His hands and His feet" v. 40

When we are resurrected (or translated if we are living when Christ returns) we will have incorruptible bodies. All natural limitations will be gone. We will have no crooked teeth, no dim eyes, no deaf ears — no scars or defects of any kind.

There will be one in our midst, however, with scars remaining. Jesus' resurrected body still had the scars placed there by our sin. For all eternity He will be the One with the scars. The one man-made thing in Heaven will be the scars in our Savior's hands, feet and side placed there by my sin and yours.

See also: Job 19:25-27, 1 Cor. 15:53-54, Phil. 3:20-21, Heb. 10:25, Rev. 5:5-6

December 16
Read John 20:24-29

"Unless I see in His hands the mark of the nails, and place my finger into the mark of the nails, and place my hand into His side, I will never believe" v. 25

The producer of an animated movie was being interviewed about his new creation. When asked if he thought people would come to see a movie in which nothing is real, he sneered and said, "Now what in any of the movies is real?" Sadly, we are living in a generation that doesn't know the difference between reality and make-believe.

When Thomas was told by eye witnesses that Jesus had risen from the dead, he refused to believe. To his credit, he did not want to live in a make-believe world. He wanted to face reality no matter how stark it may be.

Is the truth of the risen Christ in our midst a living reality to you or is it as a fable that you accept because others have conjured up the idea in their minds?

See also: Heb. 11:1, 1 Pet. 1:8

December 17
Read John 20:24-29

"Eight days later, the disciples were inside again, and Thomas was with them. Although the doors were locked, Jesus came in and stood among them" v. 26

The first time Jesus revealed Himself to His disciples, Thomas was not with them. Consequently, he missed the blessing of seeing the risen Lord. In spite of doubt and unbelief, Thomas met with his fellow disciples. Now, again gathered with the others, he saw!

Where is Jesus going to manifest Himself? In the presence of other believers, of course. During a time of questioning and unbelief it is very natural not to want to fellowship with other believers. But that is the time we need fellowship the most. And that is the time God will do the greatest work in our lives.

Maybe you are not presently attending church because of a setback in your life. If you will again begin fellowshipping with God's people, Jesus will again manifest Himself to you anew.

See also: Ps. 121:1-2, Ps. 122:1, Ps.

December 18
Read Matthew 28:16-20

"**Go therefore and make disciples of all nations, baptizing them in the name of the Father and of the Son and of the Holy Spirit, teaching them to observe all that I have commanded you**" v. 19 [November Memory Verse]

Jesus' final command to His disciples is commonly called the Great Commission. It is said that His last command should be our first concern. For many, however, the great commission has become the great omission. But it is just as binding on us today as it was for His original disciples.

In Matthew 28:16-20, Jesus' final command, He used the word 'all' four times: 1. <u>All authority</u> — He took authority over disease, demons, and death. Now He takes authority over His disciples and gives them a command. 2. <u>All nations</u> — His message was for every man, woman, boy, girl, tribe and nation that has ever lived or ever will live. 3. <u>All things</u> — Everything He has taught us, we are to teach to others. 4. <u>Always</u> present — We are not alone. He is with us right now!

In the final analysis, a disciple is one who is making disciples. Is His last command your first concern?

See also: Hab. 2:14, Acts 26:19

December 19
Read Matthew 28:16-20

"**And behold, I am with you always, to the end of the age**" v. 20

Late one sunny afternoon, my seven year old daughter and I went for a bike ride. The trip took us down an alley, behind the post office, across the railroad tracks, past the old depot and up a side-road she had never been on before. She was not at all familiar with where she was. But she said confidently, "I don't know where we are, but I'm not afraid, because I'm with you."

God assures us that as we go out on a divine purpose, we also have divine presence. Often as we travel the many roads and turns of this life, we really are not sure where we are. But we can always know who is with us. His promise is to be with us "to the end of the age." Amen.

See also: Ex. 33:14, Deut. 31:6, Phil. 4:9

December 20
Read Mark 16:14-20

"And He said to them, 'Go into all the world and proclaim the gospel to the whole creation'" v. 15

Former president of the United Nations General Assembly, Dr. Charles Malik, said, "The greatest thing to come out of America has been the American missionary effort: the quiet, selfless men and women who left the comfort of their homeland to bring the Gospel of Christianity to less fortunate nations."

The reason the church exists is to fulfill the Great Commandment and the Great Commission. Indeed, the modern missionary movement has influenced our world more than most people realize. Those who have gone are literally fulfilling Christ's last command. If you know someone who has left our shores to take the Gospel to other lands, that person deserves your support both financially and in prayer. Why not stop and pray for that person right now?

See also: Hab. 2:14, Rom. 10:18

December 21
Read Mark 16:14-18

"Whoever believes and is baptized will be saved" v. 16

There are two baptisms — a physical baptism and spiritual baptism. When a person is baptized spiritually, he is placed into Christ. Being inside of Christ, we have already been spiritually crucified, buried, and raised to newness of life! This happens the moment we believe. Baptism by immersion signifies being buried with Christ as we are put into the water and being raised with Christ as we come out of the water. Thus we can live on the resurrection side of the grave right here and right now! This is a truth that many Christians never grasp. The Apostle Paul expressed this reality when he said that he was crucified with Christ (Galatians 2:20).

You are inside of Christ. Christ is inside of you. Putting these two truths into practice will revolutionize your life. It really will!

See also: Rom. 6:1-11, Col. 3:1-4

December 22
Read Luke 24:44-49

"Repentance and forgiveness of sins should be proclaimed in His name to all nations beginning from Jerusalem" v. 47

Christ has left His followers with a message and a mission.

Our message is that The Christ suffered for our sins and arose from the dead. This is the greatest story ever heard by human ear and the basis of our salvation.

Our mission is to the remotest parts of the earth. A faithful follower of Christ will carry His message to every street and alley of every city in the world.

The message of Christ has been faithfully carried from one generation to the next until this very hour. We are the recipients of the work of faithful believers who went before us. Now the torch is in our hands. We may be the generation that experiences Christ's return. If so, we need to be faithful to finish the job He commissioned us to do.

Is there someone that Christ will have you share His dying /undying love with today?

See also: Rom. 10:14-15, 2 Cor. 5:18-20

December 23
Read Luke 24:44-49

"You are witnesses of these things" v. 48

Some Christians want to be lawyers, analyzing every word of others. Others want to be judges, condemning every flaw they see. We are not called to be lawyers or judges, but witnesses. A witness is someone who can give a first-hand account of an event. Anyone giving a hearsay account in a court of law would quickly be discredited.

The event we are to give witness to is the resurrection of Jesus Christ. We are called to testify to a first-hand encounter of meeting the resurrected Christ. If you cannot do that, you need someone to witness to you.

See also: Acts 10:42, Acts 20:20-24, 1 Jn. 4:14, Rev. 12:11

December 24
Read Mark 16:19-20

"They went out and preached everywhere, while the Lord worked with them" v. 20

The Lord still speaks audibly today —through people —through my voice and yours. He still loves today — through us. He still works today — through me and you. If God is going to do anything in this world, He will do it through His people. The Spirit of God speaks the word of God through the man of God. That is His primary method of communicating to this world. Our job is to obey. As we do, we can be certain that the Lord is working with us.

Extra: Christmas is when the Son of God became the Son of Man so the sons of men might become sons of God!

See also: Acts 5:32, Acts 8:4, 1 Thess. 1:8

December 25
Read John 20:30-31

"These are written so that you may believe that Jesus is the Christ, the Son of God, and that by believing you may have life in His name" v. 31
[December Memory Verse]

"Believe" is written 93 times in the book of John. The thing John first wants us to believe is not what Jesus did but who He is. The result of believing will be having—having eternal life. These two words, 'believe' and ' have' are the same two verbs used in John 3:16.

The key word throughout the Gospel of John is 'believe'. The key word in John's epistle is 'know'. ' Believe' changes to 'know'! Has *believe* changed to *know* in your life? Is there an unshakable certainty that you have eternal life? There can be.

PS. "...have life in His name" — What a Christmas gift!

See also: 2 Tim. 1:12, 1 Jn. 5:13

December 26
Read John 21:15-17

"Simon, son of John, do you love Me more than these?" v. 15

There is something about the number three that seals the deal. If you do something three times, a pattern has been established. If you say something three times, it is considered an established fact.

Three times Peter denied Jesus. Three times Jesus asked, "Do you love Me?" And notice who Jesus was addressing—Not Peter, the rock, but Simon, sifting sand (his name before he became a follower of Jesus—John 1:42). How quickly we revert to our old lifestyle when we deny our Lord.

After Simon responded to Jesus' question, Jesus said, "Feed My lambs… Tend My sheep…Feed My sheep". The test of our love for Jesus is our care for other followers of Christ.

See also: Deut. 6:5, 1 Jn. 5:1-3

December 27
Read John 21:18-23

"Peter turned and saw the disciple whom Jesus loved following them… When Peter saw him, he said to Jesus, 'Lord, what about this man?'" v. 20-21

Tradition says that Peter was crucified in Rome in fulfillment of Jesus' prophecy in verse 18. But he was crucified upside down because he said he was not worthy to be crucified as his Savior was.

But what about John? What about the guy who has it better than you? What about the guy who has an easier life than you? What about the guy who is not enduring the trials you are? Jesus would kindly but firmly say to you, as He said to Peter, "What is that to you?" (v. 22). He has called you to a task. He has called you to a mission. And what He calls someone else to is between that person and God. So let us each be willing to carry our own cross and not worry about God's call on other people's lives.

PS. John was the only disciple not to be martyred for Christ. God spared him from martyrdom so he could write the book of Revelation—providence at work again!

See also: Acts 9:15-16, 2 Pet. 1:13-15

December 28
Read Acts 1:1-3

"In the first book, O Theophilus, I have dealt with all that Jesus began to do and teach until the day when He was taken up…" v. 1-2

When the Bible was originally written it did not have chapters and verses. While chapter and verse divisions make it very easy for referencing, they are not necessarily inspired by God. Here is a good example of a verse being divided in the wrong place.

Jesus came to earth, died for our sins, rose from the dead, ascended to Heaven. That was the end of the beginning! During Jesus life in the flesh He began to do and teach many things. But it was not completed. Even the book of Acts ends without an ending! (Check it out). Christ's work continues today not in His physical body but by His Spirit. The Lord Jesus Christ who was born in Bethlehem is at work through His church around the world right now! The work will not end until the church reaches its full stature and Christ returns. This is God's agenda for this present age.

See also: Eph. 4:13, Eph. 5:27, Rev. 19:7

December 29
Read Acts 1:1-8

"For John baptized with water, but you will be baptized with the Holy Spirit not many days from now" v. 5

The Holy Spirit is given for two reasons — victorious living and effective service.

In Acts 2:39, Peter tells us who the Holy Spirit is given to — 1. You (You know who 'you' are, don't you?) 2. Your children (God has big plans for the next generation! …Really <u>BIG</u> plans!) 3. All who are far off (All means all.) 4. Everyone whom the Lord our God calls to Himself.

The coming of the Holy Spirit is a literal historical event that never needs to be repeated any more than Jesus needs to be crucified or raised again. The Holy Spirit with all His power is here right now. The same Spirit that indwelt Jesus indwells you! We have the commands. We have the promises. We have the power of the Holy Spirit as we obey. Let us go forward in His name that He may work through us.

See also: Acts 2:38-39, Acts 5:32

December 30
Read Acts 1:6-11

"Men of Galilee, why do you stand looking into Heaven? This Jesus, who was taken up from you into Heaven, will come in the same way as you saw Him go into Heaven" v. 11

We often hear of space probes to other planets to find life. Personally I think it is all an effort to substantiate evolution and discredit our Creator. But we find more life in one square foot of land or water here than we have found on all the distant objects of outer space we have reached.

Is there life beyond this planet? There certainly is spiritual life, for we read of myriads of angelic beings in heavenly realms. But I question if there is physical or natural life. Even if there were, it would need to be a pretty special place to top our earth!

Earth is indeed special. First, because of all the diverse forms of life it has. Second, because this is the planet we call home. Third, this is the place where Jesus, the Creator of all things, has visited. And fourth, this is the place from which He will rule the universe in the future.

The return of Jesus to earth is as certain as His resurrection. Keep looking toward the Mount of Olives!

See also: Dan. 2:44, Zech. 14:4, Rev. 1:7, Rev. 11:15

December 31
Read John. 21:24-25

"Now there are also many other things that Jesus did. Were every one of them to be written, I suppose that the world itself could not contain the books that would be written" v. 25

More books have been written about or inspired by the Lord Jesus than any other person in history. And you have just finished reading another one! But this book was not intended to be a substitute for the Bible but a supplement to it.

Through the writing of this book, I have come to appreciate anew the four Gospels and the magnificent Life that inspired them. I urge you to daily read your Bible. Study it, memorize it, meditate on it, write it out. Do word studies. Use different translations. Spend time digging for precious gems. May you truly see Jesus on its pages. Make it your life's ambition to learn of Him. Don't lose the wonder of your magnificent Savior. And don't lose the beauty of His Book.

"Now to Him who is able to keep you from stumbling and to present you blameless before the presence of His glory with great joy, to the only God, our Savior, through Jesus Christ our Lord be glory, majesty, dominion, and authority, before all time and now and forever. Amen." (Jude 1:24-25) I'll C-U there!

See also: Josh. 1:8, Ps. 1:1-3, Ps. 19:7-11

"'I am the Alpha and the Omega' says the Lord God, 'who is and who was and who is to come, The Almighty'"
Revelation 1:8

"Fear not, I am the first and the last and the living One. I died, and behold I am alive forevermore, and I have the keys of death and Hades"
Revelation 1:17-18

"Behold, I am coming soon, bringing My recompense with Me to repay everyone for what he has done"
Revelation 22:12

Jesus, Jesus:	Name above all names, Age to age the same.
Savior, Savior:	Took away my sin, Made me clean within.
Shepherd, Shepherd:	Ever faithful Friend, With me to the end.
Master, Master:	Wisdom from above, Filled with truth and love.
Healer, Healer:	All Your mighty power, For this day, this hour.
Holy, Holy:	Holy are You, Lord, In highest Heaven adored.
Father, Father:	Make me more like you, Pure and just and true.

WEEKLY BIBLE MEMORY PLAN — THE GOSPELS
* Monthly Memory Plan

Month	Week	Verse	Month	Week	Verse
Jan.	1	Jn. 1:1-3	July	1	Jn. 8:12
	2	Mt. 1:21		2	Jn. 8:31-32
	3	Jn. 1:12 *		3	Jn. 10:10
	4	Jn. 1:29		4	Jn. 10:27-28 *
	5	Mt. 4:4		5	Jn. 11:25-26
Feb.	1	Mt. 4:17	Aug.	1	Lk. 15:10
	2	Mt. 4:19		2	Lk. 16:13
	3	Jn. 3:16-17 *		3	Lk. 19:10 *
	4	Jn. 4:10		4	Mk. 12:30-31
Mar.	1	Jn. 4:23	Sep.	1	Mt. 18:20
	2	Jn. 5:24 *		2	Mt. 24:14
	3	Mt. 5:14-16		3	Lk. 21:33
	4	Mt. 6:24		4	Jn. 13:34-35 *
Apr	1	Mt. 6:33 *	Oct.	1	Jn. 14:1-3
	2	Mt. 7:13-14		2	Jn. 14:6 *
	3	Mt. 10:16		3	Jn. 14:21
	4	Jn. 6:35		4	Jn. 14:27
May	1	Jn. 6:68-69		5	Jn. 15:5
	2	Mt. 11:28-29 *	Nov.	1	Jn. 15:7
	3	Mt. 12:36-37		2	Lk. 23:34
	4	Mk. 8:36-37		3	Jn. 15:16
	5	Mt. 16:15-16		4	Mt. 28:18-20 *
Jun.	1	Lk. 10:2	Dec.	1	Jn. 16:33
	2	Lk. 12:8		2	Jn. 17:21
	3	Lk. 14:33		3	Lk. 24:46-47
	4	Mk. 10:45 *		4	Jn. 20:31 *